Japan's Choices

Japan's Choices

New Globalism and Cultural Orientations in an Industrial State

Edited by
Professor Masataka Kosaka
Kyoto University and Chairman of the
'Japan's Choices' Study Group

Pinter Publishers
London and New York

© The Japan's Choices Study Group, 1989

First published in Great Britain in 1989 by
Pinter Publishers Limited
25 Floral Street, London WC2E 9DS

British Library Cataloguing in Publication Data
A CIP catalogue record for this book is available from the British Library
ISBN 0 86187 791 8

Library of Congress Cataloging-in-Publication Data

Japan's choices.

   Includes index.
   1. Japan—Foreign economic relations. 2. Japan—
Economic policy—1945- . 3. Japan—Foreign
relations. 4. Japan—Cultural policy. I. Kosaka,
Masataka, 1934-
HF1601.J365   1989   337.52   89-8705
ISBN 0-86187-791-8

Typeset by York House Typographic Ltd, London W7
Printed and bound in Great Britain by Biddles Ltd

Contents

4: Domestic preparations for becoming a new culturally oriented industrial state   90

Appendices

Index   159

The 'Japan's Choices' Study Group

List of members

Masataka Kosaka (Chairman)	Professor of the Faculty of Law, Kyoto University
Takashi Inoguchi	Professor of the Institute of Oriental Culture, University of Tokyo
Moriya Uchida	Director of Teijin Ltd
Yutaka Kosai	President of the Japan Economic Research Center
Akira Kojima	Editorial Writer of the Nihon Keizai Shimbun Inc.
Yotaro Kobayashi	President of Fuji Xerox Co., Ltd
Kiyonobu Shimazu	Senior Managing Director and General Manager of Shearson Lehman Brothers Asia Inc., Tokyo Branch
Hideo Sugiura	Advisor of Honda Motor Co., Ltd
Tasuku Takagaki	Senior Managing Director of the Bank of Tokyo, Ltd
Hirotaka Takeuchi	Professor of the Faculty of Commerce, Hitotsubashi University
Heizo Takenaka	Associate Professor of the Faculty of Economics, Osaka University
Akihiko Tanaka	Associate Professor of the College of Arts and Science, University of Tokyo
Susumu Nishimura	Managing Director of Mitsubishi Corporation
Kenjiro Hayashi	Director of the Nomura Research Institute
Makoto Momoi	Guest Research Fellow of the Yomiuri Shimbun
Masakazu Yamazaki	Professor of the Faculty of Letters, Osaka University
Tadashi Yamamoto	President of the Japan Center for International Exchange

Basic Framework

Analysis of the current state of affairs

The international realm: Drifting toward instability and reorganization

1. Instability in the world economic order

2. Progress toward a new industrial revolution

3. Globalization of economic communities and lessened importance of national boundaries

4. Changes in world political and military environments

Basic ideals

The 'New Globalism': Proposals for a new framework

1. A free and open international system based on economies and cultures

2. Reforms in the GATT–IMF system and the creation of a network of open relationships among nations encompassing the various subsystems; assurance of voluntary participation by all Asian and Pacific nations

3. Application of flexible rules to diverse situations

4. The opening of Japan: Becoming a major importer and contributing to the redress of world imbalances

The domestic realm: Japan at a turning point in its history

1. Transformation to major power status accompanied by domestic and international imbalances

2. New areas of friction

3. Changing society searches for new sense of values

'The new culturally oriented industrial state': Choices for Japan's future

1. Security guarantees through linkage-based systems

2. Developing economic and technological strength and contributing to the international order

3. Devising a new style of industry, daily life and culture (promoting creativity)

Concrete Policies

Concrete implementation of a new globalism

1. Japan–US economic and industrial cooperation: Semi-macro and micro policy coordination, Japan–US industrial integration, etc.

2. Cooperative development in Asia and the Pacific

3. Restoring the industrial base through currency stabilization: Reference zone and other currency stabilization measures, internationalization of the yen

4. Increased flow of international capital: Expanded trade insurance, etc.

5. Measures to deal with trans-national corporate activities: Creation of international rules governing multinational corporations; international integration of industrial policies and corporate activities

6. The opening of Japanese society

Responses to international changes

1. Providing a 'market': Becoming a major importer

2. Providing 'capital': Economic cooperation based on a tripartite strategy of assistance, trade, and investment

3. Providing 'technology': Becoming a center of creative knowledge through technology disclosure; creating new rules for intellectual property rights

Restoration of the domestic base

1. Economic management designed to redress domestic and international imbalances

2. Institutional reforms to promote greater creativity

3. Increased scholarly and basic research activities: Promoting R & D investments as a new form of social capital; reforms to cultivate a freer and more creative research environment

4. Fostering economic growth in areas outside major cities

Preface

The postwar world environment has undergone dramatic changes and a new order is about to emerge. In the economic sphere, a relative decline in the position of the US economy has destabilized the international economic order. In the areas of industry and technology, the current wave of technical innovations has brought about a new industrial revolution leading the world economic community into uncharted territory.

In addition, with the globalization of economic activity, national borders have lost their significance. It has become extremely difficult to reconcile pursuing an internationally open economic society with protecting domestic interests under the traditional nation-state framework. In the political and military arenas, rapid improvements in US-Soviet relations are dramatically changing the structure of postwar international politics, placing far greater importance on the role of the economy and technology as elements of national strength.

Amidst these changes in the world order, Japan stands at a turning point in its own history. It has passed all other developed countries in per capita GDP, and has also become the world's largest creditor nation. These and other events demonstrate that Japan has achieved the status of a major power, a development that demands responsible steps on Japan's part. International friction involving Japan poses fundamental problems for Japanese society, involving as it does conflict with institutions rooted in differences in lifestyle and culture. In this context, Japanese society confronts demands both from within and without to create a new and distinctive style (and sense of values) in industry, daily life and culture. The Japanese people increasingly seek not only material wealth but also psychological richness and a profound spiritual sensitivity. They are now taking the first real steps, despite the current confusion, to search for new values.

Recognizing these changes in the world and Japan, Shinji Fukukawa former Administrative Vice-Minister for International Trade and Industry convened the 'Japan's Choices' Study Group. The group discussed these issues during eleven meetings held between October 1987 and May 1988. The members of the group were seventeen experts from various fields and the discussions were very fruitful. As a chairman of the group, I am pleased that our collective efforts led to the report described in the pages that follow. We hope this report will lead to further discussions at various levels.

Professor Masataka Kosaka

Kyoto University and Chairman of the 'Japan's Choices' Study Group

1 Japan at a historical turning point

1. Turmoil and reconstruction in the international order

The postwar international order is currently undergoing sweeping changes in the fields of economics, politics, and military affairs, and there are indications that a new order is on the horizon.

(1) The world economic system in turmoil

There is currently considerable turmoil in the world economic system. The foundation of the postwar international economic order was formed by the establishment of the General Agreement on Tariffs and Trade (GATT) and the International Monetary Fund (IMF) system. These organizations were founded on the basic principle of a free and nondiscriminatory world economy. This order came about under the leadership and support of the United States. From an economic standpoint the relative position of the United States has slipped in recent years, although there are currently some signs of renewal in America, such as the recovery in exports as a result of the fall of the dollar. Nevertheless, the enormous twin deficits and the country's new status as a debtor nation have drastically weakened the ability of the United States to support a free and international economic system.

Despite problems such as the high unemployment rate among young people in Europe, the situation there is less bleak. The European Community (EC) has continued to move forward with plans to unify the market in 1992. In addition, Europe is trying to activate its economy by promoting plans for structural adjustments, deregulation and the development of new technologies.

As for the developing countries, they are struggling under the burdens of a long-term slump in prices for primary products and an accumulating debt. Moreover, the gap between the north and the south continues to widen, with no clear prospects for balanced economic development in sight.

In contrast to this, Newly Industrialized Countries (NICs) such as Korea and Taiwan are chalking up remarkable growth rates, and members of the Association of South East Asian Nations (ASEAN) as a whole are also showing signs of getting on track. Coupled with Japan's expansion and China's open-door policies, these developments point to the dynamic nature of economic expansion in the Asia/Pacific region.

Turning to the Eastern Bloc, the partial introduction of market mechanisms and attempts to participate in the world economic system on the part of the Soviet Union and the East European nations constitute serious efforts toward reform which should impart new vigour to the stagnating economies of these countries.

The world economy is today faced with the problem of enormous imbalances. The foundation for healthy expansion is being jeopardized by the American trade deficit, trade surpluses in countries such as Japan, West Germany and some of the Asian NICs, the rapid accumulation of debt in the United States, and the expanding accumulation of debt in Central and South American nations. If solid measures to correct these imbalances are not taken, disorder in the international financial system and a rise in protectionism could plunge the world economy into chaos.

However, a variety of trends are becoming evident in attempts to find a new direction in managing the global economy. For example:

(i)   There is a tendency toward strengthening the existing international economic management system through cooperation on the part of the developed countries to complement US economic leadership. There has been a rapid strengthening over the past few years of efforts toward management of the global economy through coordinated policies of the leading nations, such as summits, Group of Five (G5) and Group of Seven (G7) talks, and quadripartite trade minister conferences.

(ii)   As evidenced by the Paraguay Round of GATT, efforts are being made to reform the postwar GATT and IMF systems and make them function more effectively and with greater adaptability.

(iii) The US-Canada Free Trade Agreement and the market unification of the EC have shown that efforts are being made to further solidify free trade systems in specific regions, and to impart new vigour to the economies of these areas. On the other hand, there is also a growing trend toward protectionism as a countermeasure against imbalances or reduced competitiveness.

In light of these developments, if the creation of a new system of cooperation does not proceed in the future, it is quite possible that protectionism and the formation of blocs could result in a situation which will jeopardize the world economic system. In this sense, it is clear that the world economy is truly at a crossroads.

(2) The new industrial revolution

The repercussions of the current technological revolution are bringing about a new industrial revolution and introducing a new dimension into the international economic community.

Major driving forces behind current technological changes are the rapid progress of engineering at the atomic or molecular level, new technological developments in a variety of fields due to the enhanced interplay between science and engineering, and the development of new technologies due to the fusion of disparate technological fields. Particularly noteworthy are the revolutionary developments in the fields of new materials, microelectronics, biotechnology, including the elucidation and application of biological functions, and superconductor technology. As a result, the traditional division of technology into areas such as metals, chemistry, machinery, electronics, electricity and textiles, has rapidly become obsolete. It has now become necessary to establish technological systems based on new principles of engineering and technology.

From a historical viewpoint, the powerful new technological revolution can be compared to the first technological revolution in which the development of the steam engine and coal and steel technology triggered the industrial revolution of the seventeeth and eighteenth centuries. It can also be compared to the second technological revolution, in which developments in electric power, telecommunications, automobile, internal combustion engine and petroleum technology drastically changed the late nineteenth and twentieth centuries.

The current technological revolution should cause reforms in production and management methods that will give rise to a variety of new products and new industries. It is thought that the advent of new products and services will simultaneously bring about sweeping changes in people's lifestyles, consciousness and sense of values.

In the long term, the steps taken to meet this new industrial revolution will be the key factors affecting future expansion of the economic community and a driving force in the world economy. At the same time, there is a possibility that the expanding technological revolution may further aggravate problems between the north and south. In any event, the international repercussions of these new technologies and industrial revolution will no doubt result in the construction of a new framework.

(3) Change in the significance of national borders

The definition of national borders is changing as the globalization of economic activity proceeds. The explosive expansion of transportation, communications and information technology, and deregulation on a worldwide scale are resulting in an internationalization of corporate activity and a deepening of economic interdependency. These trends should become more pronounced in the future. In particular, the rapid growth in Japanese direct investment abroad since the recent appreciation of the yen has resulted in aggressive development of global management structures which transcend national borders. As a result of such activities, the concept of national borders is rapidly changing.

The globalization of economic activity has made it impossible to push ahead with economic development within the limited framework of a country defined by strict national borders. International harmony with respect to the framework of various systems which support economic activity, beginning with the tax system, is becoming increasingly vital. The rationality, effectiveness and universality of the various systems a country has at its disposal to support economic activity have come to have an enormous impact on that country's prosperity. It is becoming increasingly important for the systems of various countries to be international in nature.

On the other hand, although national economic barriers are clearly being diminished, national borders are still the most important framework for regulating economic activity and private life, and this should remain unchanged in the future. The state still plays a considerable role in ensuring the welfare of its citizens by protecting the economically weak, stabilizing society, consolidating a foundation for cultural development, and maintaining an identity. The degree to which it is possible to reconcile the pursuit of economic rationality tailored to the globalization of economic activity and the opening-up of the economic society to other nations with the protection of social interests within a national framework has become an extremely difficult problem.

(4) Changes in global political and military environments

Broad changes are sweeping the environment surrounding world political and military relations. For instance, US-Soviet relations have taken a turn for the better, and with the Intermediate Nuclear Forces (INF) agreement, signs of a new *détente* have begun to appear. Thus major changes are taking place in the postwar international political framework which has been based on the bipolar opposition between these two superpowers. Both the United States and the Soviet Union are becoming increasingly aware of the dangers of a direct confrontation in the form of a nuclear war, and the emphasis in military strategy has shifted to peripheral or third-party countries. In addition, as structural changes connected with the *rapprochement* between the United States and the Soviet Union take place, conflicts taking place in areas such as Europe, Asia, the Middle East, and Central and South America have also taken on a new aspect. In light of this, the superpowers have focused increased attention on the role of the economy in security matters – particularly the role of high-level technology in supporting the military establishment – and a shift in national priorities toward economics and technology is now taking place in these countries.

Furthermore, as can be seen by US demands for greater defense burden sharing and economic cooperation with respect to Japan and Europe, a reorganization and adjustment of relations among Western nations is proceeding, as these countries search for a new balance.

2. Toward becoming a major power: new friction

Changes in the world order described above have affected the course of economic expansion followed by Japan up to the present and have brought it to the threshold of a historical turning point.

(1) Issues connected with Japan's new status as a major power

Japan has encountered a variety of turning points in the course of its modernization since the Meiji era (1868–1912). However, the problems currently facing Japan involve changes in several internal and external frameworks, and as such are fundamentally different from the problems of the past.

The position held by Japan in the world economy has risen very rapidly. It has already been several years since Japan was referred to as the country accounting for 10 per cent of the world's economy. Japan's gross domestic product (GDP) now accounts for 15 per cent of the world's total production. In terms of per capita GDP, Japan has overtaken the United States and West Germany and now holds the number-one slot among the world's main industrialized countries. Furthermore, while the United States has slipped to the status of a debtor nation, Japan has become the world's top creditor country, with net foreign claims of some $180 billion as of the end of 1986.

Japan's enormous current-account surplus has taken on such proportions that it might shake the foundations of healthy world economic development. It should be noted that the main factors behind the present surplus lie with the deficit countries rather than with the surplus countries. However, when one considers the long-term development of the world economy, which has a prerequisite for its prosperity, Japan cannot continue to have an enormous surplus forever. That is why the surplus countries should make efforts to correct the imbalance, in addition to the efforts which need to be made by the deficit countries. For its own sake as well, Japan should fulfil its responsibilities as a surplus country. Although, in fact, Japan is now making efforts to reduce its surplus by making adjustments in the domestic economic structure and by expanding its imports, these efforts will have to be continued in the future.

Indeed, as Japan has become a major economic power, the measures it takes have come to have an extremely strong impact on the global economy. But it is difficult for the average Japanese citizen to understand the extent of this new influence because this country has not yet reached the level of the West with respect to such factors as commodity prices, working hours, housing, land, social capital and personal exchanges. In many ways, Japan remains a small country in terms of richness and quality of life. It goes without saying that the gap between Japan's current position as a major economic power and the actual quality of everyday life in the country will have to be eliminated as quickly as possible by increasing investments and reforming various systems relating to individual standards of living. This is one of the most important problems currently facing Japan.

Japan must therefore squarely confront its new status by shouldering its share of the burden and continuing to take responsible steps for the purpose of promoting international development. (See Appendix 1: Per capita GDP in advanced industrialized nations.)

(2) Changes in and new aspects of friction with other countries

In considering Japan's path in the world, it is of vital importance to be aware both of the country's new status as an economic power and of how the content and nature of friction between Japan and other countries have changed.

CHANGES IN FRICTION

Economic friction between Japan and other countries began with exports. These problems involved textiles and miscellaneous goods in the 1960s, steel and color televisions in the 1970s, and industrial products, such as automobiles, machine tools and semiconductors, in the 1980s. Moreover, friction involving exports has recently been joined by increasing import-related tension. This involves the problems of opening up Japanese markets, and demands have been made to open up the finance, communications, agricultural products, construction, spirits and tobacco markets. At the same time, the problems of opening up markets have moved from 'waterfront' problems such as customs and import restrictions to 'inland' concerns such as distribution and business practices. Problems connected with Japanese social and cultural values and habits, such as savings consciousness and long working hours, as well as the problems of intellectual property rights and technological development policies, have also recently become sources of friction.

THREE TYPES OF FRICTION WITH FOREIGN COUNTRIES AND RELATED COUNTERMEASURES

The friction currently faced by Japan can be divided into roughly three types, in terms of the degree of difficulty in devising appropriate countermeasures.

The first type of friction can be dealt with if efforts are made to form a popular consensus; both the government and the general public are closely involved; and a combination of appropriate domestic and foreign policies are implemented. This involves reforming the system with respect to friction in individual industries, easing regulations, as well as shortening working hours.

The second type of friction involves social customs and individual lifestyles, and it will take time to deal with. This has to do with business practices, the distribution system and safety regulations. This variety has a longer history than the first type, and as it entails the problems which are based on social standards, dealing with it will be no easy matter.

The third type, friction that may develop in the future as a result of cultural differences, is also a consideration, and it too will be an extremely difficult problem to solve. Examples of this are friction involving the Japanese system of management, which is centered on the employee, and peculiarities in the legal system arising from cultural differences. This will test the universality and international receptivity of Japanese culture. It is important that Japan maintain an appreciation of the validity of its own value standards. In order for Japan to be accepted into the world community, however, it is also necessary that it discern where international value standards lie and assume a posture of flexibility incorporating appropriate international standards. Furthermore, it will be necessary to deal with the friction by aggressively creating independent new values and forms of industry, daily life and culture which are attractive and applicable to the international community.

The fact that there is not only the first type of friction with foreign countries, but that this friction is expanding to include the second and third types, is further proof that Japan stands at a historic turning point. (See Appendix 2: Trade friction issues, images of Japan and possible Japanese responses.)

3. Transformation of Japanese society and the search for new values

Japan is faced at present with the problem of having to construct new styles (or values and forms) of industry, daily life and culture.

Instead of an outside demand by the international community, this is something which is being sought from within Japanese society itself, and is an issue which Japan will absolutely have to deal with in order to proceed into the twenty-first century.

More and more, Japanese people are seeking a lifestyle which is not only physically complete but also spiritually whole. The most urgent issue is that of filling the gap between the country's economic strength, as expressed by the GNP, and actual standards of living in order to become a truly affluent nation. This applies not only to material abundance but also spiritual abundance. It is also manifested in the increasing desire for free time, increasing cultural needs involving lifelong education, fine arts, music, plays and books, an increasing orientation toward health and nature, and the demand for versatile information which helps expand the scope of individual choice. The change in product-purchasing attitudes of consumers from the 'functional orientation,' which emphasizes performance, to the 'sensitivity orientation,' which emphasizes color and design, and further to the 'emotional orientation,' which emphasizes personal contact in services, cannot be ignored.

Second, in response to the demand-side changes in the consciousness of consumers, changes are also taking place on the supply side with respect to industry. This can be seen in trends such as the appearance of various types of new businesses, the development of new products which see added value in individuality, and 'high-touch' orientation, and the revolution in and diversification of means of communication due to the new electronic media.

However, it can be said that, generally speaking, both consumers and industry are unable to grasp the new lifestyle images at the forefront of the changes currently taking place. In order to reach its goal of achieving a standard of living comparable to that in Europe and the United States, Japanese industry has so far emphasized the social utility of industrial products and expressed confidence that, as an innovator, it can improve consumer lifestyles. In fact, it has continually provided society with products, such as electrical appliances, automobiles and computers. However, with the current diversification of consumer needs, a search for new goals and a new industrial philosophy has begun. Generally, new styles (values and forms) of industry, daily life and culture are formed from the interaction of the diversified 'selections,' which spring from the needs of the people themselves, and the diversified 'proposals' made by industry. The current situation is still marked by chaos, but one can say that steady progress towards the formation of new styles is becoming apparent amidst the current social changes.

4. An important juncture: new directions

Prosperous countries can be characterized by various political, military, economic and cultural elements, and, in general, they have striven for economic and cultural development under the aegis of political and military power. Nevertheless, the global relationship between socioeconomic factors and military/political ones is currently becoming more relaxed, with the role that political and military power plays in determining the socioeconomic framework receding. On the contrary, as can be seen in the free nations, the trend toward supporting more healthy political and military affairs through free economic and cultural development is causing a major turnaround. In addition, the world can be said to be undergoing a transformation of national borders from an order of 'territorial hegemony,' in which nations and communities are divided by territory, to an order of 'mutual permeation' characterized by free exchange centering on industry and culture.

These factors can be characterized as historically unprecedented environmental changes which create greater opportunities for Japan to expand its influence.

Given the transformations taking place in the world order, and severe frictions with the international community, as Japan is faced with its new status as a major power, it may have to select the following course in the future.

(1) The 'new globalism' and Japan's role

First, Japan must make efforts towards the formation of a new world order in the spirit of a 'new globalism.' The essential points of this new globalism are as follows.

Based on the changing interrelationship between military/political and socioeconomic factors, it is necessary to form a system of solidarity among nations centering on economics and culture. This involves placing a high value on free and open economic and cultural exchange at the global level, as a means for creating a healthier world political climate and bringing about stabilization and expansion of the world economy.

In order to increase the utility of the system of international organizations such as GATT, the Organization for Economic Cooperation and Development (OECD) and the IMF, Japan must make efforts to revitalize such organizations (for example, through promotion of the Uruguay Round of GATT), as well as to form various types of open groupings of nations as a subsystem supporting multilateralism.

To be more specific, it is necessary to try and strengthen US–Japan economic and industrial cooperation with a view toward recovering and maintaining US influence on the world economic order (that is, a US–

Japan alignment); the formation of a new division of labor centering on the Pacific Rim (alignment of the United States, Japan and the Asian/ Pacific countries); maintenance of the trilateral open system and policy cooperation among Japan, the United States and Europe (alignment of Japan, the United States and Europe); and also the construction of a new cooperative relationship among countries in Central and South America, the Middle East, and Africa on the one hand, and the industrialized nations on the other. In this case, it is indispensable that these various alignments be open to non-participating countries as well. With a subsystem of accumulated and stratified open relations among nations, it is also necessary to reconstruct a global 'free world' economic system.

The role of Japan, the United States and Europe in supporting the world economic order is great, but it is necessary to seek the participation of Asia/Pacific countries as well, and to strive for an appropriate center of gravity which can support the world economic order.

In forming international codes in the future, Japan must try to avoid the uniform application of the rules of the developed nations and select flexible rules which take into consideration the diversified stages and forms of development of other nations. In order to make globalism function usefully, it is essential that a liberal and tolerant strategy be established which takes into account the considerations of various countries.

It is vital that Japan open up to foreign countries by using its own reforms as an example for the new globalism. It must revise its formerly lopsided direction of internationalization involving financial, capital, personnel, and corporate outflows from Japan, and adopt a 'balanced internationalism' which promotes inflows into Japan from abroad. In concrete terms, while striving to become a major import nation by expanding product imports and opening up markets, Japan must also aggressively promote an opening up toward foreign countries by fostering the participation and personal exchanges of foreign companies. In so doing, Japan can help redress international economic imbalances and make contributions toward development.

Japan must also open up to the world in science and technology by advocating and implementing new rules in the field of intellectual property. This will help bring about a rejuvenation of the world economy by taking full advantage of new technological and industrial revolutions.

The following are examples of policy issues which should be swiftly undertaken and implemented by Japan in connection with the spirit of the new globalism.

(i)   To strengthen economic and industrial cooperation between Japan and the United States requires more than strengthening macroeconomic policy cooperation. Japan must also establish 'semi-macroeconomic' policy cooperation, such as industrial adjustment, and harmonize Japanese and American industry, which means promoting transfers of production technology and administrative methods through Japanese investments in the United States.

(ii)   From the viewpoint of promoting development of the Asia/Pacific region, Japan must strive to foster mutual understanding and cooperation by promoting industrial cooperation among these countries and creating a forum for dialogue on important policy and other issues.

(iii)   Japan must extend trade insurance in order to expand the international recycling of funds; promote environmental consolidation through studies and policy cooperation on an international currency system (including reference zones), which would contribute to industrial stimulation based on currency stabilization; and promote internationalization of the yen.

(iv)   For economic activity which transcends national borders, it is hoped that an international code of rules with respect to jurisdiction of multinational enterprises should be established in order to clarify the status of an investing parent company in the affairs of its foreign subsidiaries. Not only a reform of individual company management strategies, but the implementation of international cooperation in corporate activity is now necessary, as is the development of international industrial policies by various countries. As national borders are transformed, it has become necessary for Japanese society to open itself up further through internationalizing its systems and personnel exchanges, while at the same time maintaining its own culture.

(2) World participation as a new culturally oriented industrial state

Second, as a 'new culturally oriented industrial state,' Japan must strive to develop and establish a framework of security based on its own system of linkages and a program of new international participation through industrial culture.

Generally, major power status has required filling four criteria: military power, political strength, economic strength and cultural universality. Of the four, Japan is a major power only in terms of economic power. In the future, as the relative weight of military power decreases in the overall framework of world affairs, Japan should opt to establish itself as a culturally oriented industrial state. In addition to its economic strength, Japan should make efforts towards the creation of a pioneering new world culture and, against this backdrop, make contributions toward world peace and development.

With the goal of securing the defense of its national territory and the free and democratic system which is the foundation of Japanese society, Japan must strive to improve its own military strength. In addition, it is necessary for Japan to increase its usefulness to the world community by expanding its contribution to international society as a whole and its relationships of mutual interdependency with foreign countries. Japan's security should be a linkage system combining the elements of military security and international interdependence.

In order for Japan to pursue development while increasing its usefulness in the international community in the future, the concepts of voluntarism, altruism and enlightened self-interest must gradually become established among the Japanese people. It will also be necessary for a multi-layer human network to be formed among the nations of the world, not only on a governmental but also on a private level.

As a new culturally oriented industrial state, Japan must establish a new framework of international cooperation which takes advantage of its market, capital, technology and culture.

(i)   Market: Japan should further open up its market to foreign countries and actively seek to eliminate global trade imbalances.

(ii)   Capital: In addition to the planned quantitative and qualitative expansion of official development assistance (ODA) for the promotion of economic cooperation, Japan must push forward with the consolidation of comprehensive domestic and foreign assistance mechanisms by training outstanding personnel in the field of international cooperation.

(iii) Technology: Based on the principle of an opening up to the world in science and technology, Japan must strive to perfect its own basic research and development in order to spur the world economy toward the new wave of industrial revolution. Japan must also work towards the creation of new rules on intellectual property rights which take into consideration the position of the NICs and developing countries.

(iv)   Culture: Japan must strive to construct creative new styles (or values and forms) of industry, daily life and culture which will be held in high esteem by foreign countries.

Considering its contributions to the world in economics and technology, Japan must strive toward appropriate management of advanced technology applicable to military purposes ('dual technology'), taking into consideration its effect on security. At the same time, Japan must take care to avoid the 'techno-nationalism' seen in some areas in order to ensure that the soil supplying the development of the economy and technology, which should be inherently free, is not impaired.

(3) Consolidation of a domestic foundation as a new culturally oriented industrial state

Third, in order to construct a domestic foundation as a new culturally oriented industrial state, Japan must carry out domestic structural reforms that would provide new styles of industry, daily life and culture – that is to say, a 'creative-type civilization.'

A new lifestyle is about to be born as a response to technological innovations (including high technology and new electronic media) and new industries that meet the changing, diverse needs of the people. The combination of this lifestyle and the society of longevity for which Japan is renowned can constitute a 'Japanese dream' that is highly regarded by people all over the world.

The Japanese system, which has been in existence since the start of the Meiji Restoration (1868), was designed so that Japan could catch up with the United States and Europe as efficiently as possible. To switch, however, from this 'catch-up' orientation to a creative-type system which places importance on the selection and responsibility of individuals, Japan must reform the overall framework of such fields as industry, society, daily life and culture. For this purpose, it is necessary to change the value assessment and source of distribution from the conventional government-led, centralized pattern to a 'double track' pattern in which individuals, companies, and public institutions all participate independently. It is also necessary to change drastically various systems with the purpose of forming a free society with a wide degree of selection, and to carry out extensive investment to consolidate the foundation for new styles of industry, daily life and culture.

Japan must push forward to perfect scientific and basic research and thereby gain a reputation as one of the world's centers of creative knowledge. To accomplish this, Japan must position research and development investments as new social capital, and strive to carry out reforms aimed at consolidating a free and creative research environment.

It will be necessary to study the reorganization of the present Tokyo-regional organization framework in order to promote balanced development of the national territory, thereby allowing the vitality and creativity of the provinces to unfold and correcting the current Tokyo-centralized system.

2 Japan's role in the new globalism

1. Turmoil in the global economic system and the outlook for a new industrial revolution

(1) Three problems in today's global economic system

Today's global economy is faced with three serious macroeconomic imbalances.

(A) CONTRADICTIONS IN THE AMERICAN ECONOMY

During the two terms of the Reagan administration, the US economy has enjoyed its longest period of peacetime economic expansion ever. At the same time, however, this apparent prosperity is wrapped in the contradiction of America's largest macroeconomic imbalance ever within the global economy.

In addition to its government deficit, the American economy is also beset by a private sector that is consuming and investing in excess of its savings. As a result, demand has moved overseas and the nation's current trade balance has shown increasing deficits since 1982. Meanwhile, overseas assets have shrunk so much that the United States became an overall debtor nation in 1985. Since then, the American net overseas debt figures have continued to grow to the point that total debt exceeded some US$400 billion at the end of 1987.

This situation used to be described as one of twin deficits – referring to the US government deficit (fiscal deficit) and the US overseas deficit (trade deficit), see Tables 2.1 and 2.2; however, since late 1986, the net assets of the US private sector have also slipped into negative figures, so that we may now speak of a 'triple deficit' afflicting the US economy.

Table 2.1 US fiscal deficit 1983–7 (US$bn.)

	1983	1984	1985	1986	1987
Fiscal deficit	−207.8	−185.3	−212.3	−221.2	−149.7

Source: US Office of Management and Budget

Table 2.2 US Trade balance, current balance and overseas debts, 1983–7 (US$bn.)*

	1983	1984	1985	1986	1987
Trade balance (FOB-CIF)	−64.2	−122.4	−133.6	−155.1	−170.3
Current balance	−46.2	−107.1	−115.1	−138.8	−154.0
Overseas debts (net)	89.4	3.5	−110.7	−269.2	−368.2

*See Appendix 3: US trends for personal savings and savings/investment balance.
Source: Statistics from the US Department of Commerce

The trade deficit has caused a shortage of capital in the United States, forcing borrowers to seek loans from foreign sources (i.e. influx of overseas capital). As long as these deficits remain, the interest payments on these foreign-based loans could conceivably cause foreign indebtedness to snowball. This would likely weaken confidence in the dollar, which continues to be the main support of the current global finance system, and since 1985 economists have seriously questioned the sustainability of the current trend.

This uncertainty regarding the sustainability of current macroeconomic conditions is likely to fuel fears of deepening turmoil in the global economic order and precipitate a rise in protectionism. Since 1985, in fact, it has led the government of the United States to devise overseas trade sanctions (on the basis of Section 301, Trade Act of 1974).

(B) ACCUMULATION OF FOREIGN DEBTS AMONG DEBTOR NATIONS

According to the World Bank, total foreign indebtedness among developing debtor nations stood at US$1.19 trillion at the end of 1987, and is expected to swell up to US$1.245 trillion by the end of 1988. This sum is nearly half the collective GNP of these developing nations and more than double the value of their annual exports of goods and services.

Moreover, since over 60 per cent of their outstanding loans are variable-interest loans, these countries are extremely vulnerable to fluctuations in interest rates. Consequently, any substantial rise in interest rates or worsening of their trade deficits can easily force such nations to default on their loan obligations, which in turn can destabilize the international finance system.

What deserves the most attention, however, is that since the debt crisis of 1982, while the Bank of America and other financial institutions have cut back on new financing and have sought to beef up their own capital to improve their corporate base (for example, influx of capital to developing countries has been less than the capital outflow since 1984), the standard of living (national income per capita) in many developing countries has declined.

Therefore, although the accumulated debts and the instability in the international finance system and among the banks supporting the system do constitute a serious problem, the most important and pressing issue here is not the finance system, but rather the question of how to improve economic growth and raise the standard of living in the debtor nations.

(c) TURMOIL IN THE INTERNATIONAL FINANCE SYSTEM

Today, most exchange transactions are based on financial transactions such as capital transactions or dealings. (In fact, exchange transactions have been estimated to exceed US$75 trillion per year worldwide, while the annual global trade total amounts to some US$2 trillion.)

Currency exchange dealings are now more strongly perceived as a type of assets trading akin to securities trading, yet any such dealings are extremely unstable and are contingent on the expectations of the currency exchange dealers themselves. Consequently, the relation between the current balance of payments and the exchange rates has become complex.

The corrective effect of current balance of payment imbalances on exchange rates that was predicted when the floating system of currency exchange was first adopted has not been as strong as expected.

To alleviate the instability in currency exchanges, the G7 nations have attempted to coordinate their policies by means of multilateral surveillance and other techniques. Although these efforts have had some beneficial effects, the advantages and disadvantages have been about equal for each nation, and thus the results have not always been effective.

MARKET REACTIONS

As mentioned earlier, today's global economic system is engulfed in some very serious problems. It was against this backdrop that October 1987's 'Black Monday' shook the global economy's foundations with a steep plunge in stock prices. This event could be taken as a warning from the securities market that the current situation of international economic instability is not sustainable. Although the dollar's value has been fluctuating from month to month according to reports concerning the US trade deficit, on the whole it has continued to lose ground against major foreign currencies.

(2) The magnitude of global economic imbalances

THE NEED FOR LARGE-SCALE ADJUSTMENTS IN THE GLOBAL ECONOMY

At the time of writing, the United States has compiled a foreign debt of about US$400 billion, and the seventeen other debtor nations have collectively amassed a debt of approximately US$460 billion. These colossal sums continue to increase each year and pose a major threat to global economic stability. Removal of this threatening trend will require either a change in course or an acknowledgement within the marketplace that the trend indeed exists.

To halt the expansion of its own indebtedness (i.e. to restore an even balance of payments), the United States is obliged to take extensive deficit-reducing measures, such as reinforcing the current trend toward a lower trade deficit by paying off foreign debts to facilitate the reduction of non-trade deficits.

A simplified, preliminary calculation of the US foreign debt problem based on constant parameters estimates that, in order simply to halt the growth of its foreign debts within ten years, the United States would need to improve its trade balance by US$20 billion per year (see Figure 2.1, Case 1). And even then its accumulated foreign debt would reach a peak of about US$1.3 trillion. Such a debt would require some US$900 billion of additional financing from capital-surplus nations. Alternatively, if US President Bush decides to put an end to foreign debt growth by the end of his term of office (i.e., about five years from now (see Figure 2.1, Case 2)), the annual trade balance would have to be improved by over US$40 billion and the United States would need S$400 billion in additional loans from creditor nations.

In either case, to improve its trade balance enough to completely eliminate the non-trade foreign deficit, the United States would have to achieve a trade surplus of US$40 billion to US$70 billion under conditions of balanced ordinary payments. Under current conditions, this means the United States would need to improve its balance of trade by the phenomenal amount of US$200 billion, and in view of the fact that the four largest surplus nations – Japan, West Germany, Taiwan and Canada – currently only have a combined surplus of about US$170 billion, it appears that the imbalance in the global economy can only be corrected by suitably large-scale adjustments.

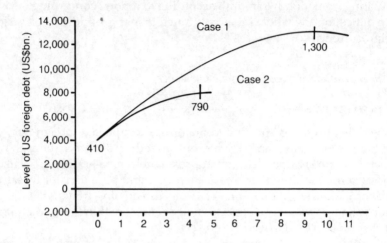

Magnitude
Case 1: Stopping debt growth in 10 years
   Initial net foreign debts: US$410 billion
   Interest: 5%
   Initial balance of payments deficit: US$150 billion
   Initial trade deficit: US$170 billion
   Required annual improvement in trade balance: US$24 billion

Case 2: Stopping debt growth in 5 years
   Initial net foreign debts: US$410 billion
   Interest: 5%
   Initial balance of payments deficit: US$150 billion
   Initial trade deficit: US$170 billion
   Required annual improvement in trade balance: US$42 billion

Impact
(Unit: US$ billion)

	Case 1	Case 2
Annual improvement in trade balance	24	42
Peak in debt accumulation	1,300	790
Amount of additional financing needed	890	380
Trade balance		
Current	−170	−170
After 5 years	−500 approx.	40 approx.
After 10 years	70	—
Trade improvement needed for equilibrium in		
balance of payments	240	210

Note: The trade balances (US$bn.) among major trade-surplus nations in 1986 are:
Japan, 92.8; West Germany, 54.7; Taiwan, 15.6; and Canada, 7.3. The total is US$
170.4 billion.

Figure 2.1 Magnitude and impact of US foreign indebtedness

POLICY RESPONSES TO CONSIDER

This movement to bring the world economy closer to equilibrium has already begun, now that the US trade deficit and Japan's trade surplus have both started to shrink. However, it would be overly optimistic to say that this slight adjustment has set a course for eliminating global imbalance. To do this, the world's nations must relinquish the pursuit of what is simply most advantageous to themselves and must instead devise powerful policy responses, such as those outlined below, that will ensure the maintenance and further development of the global economic system.

(a) Strengthening policy coordination
Today's large volume of trade and capital flow is deepening the interdependence of nations within the global economic system, such that it is now very difficult for the economic policies of any one nation to correct the considerable imbalances alone in this system. Such corrections will instead require a substantial strengthening of coordination in policy-making among debtor nations such as the United States and creditor nations such as Japan and West Germany.

It is also very important that these nations promote policy coordination that sets common goals not only at the macroeconomic level, such as in finance and government budgeting, but also at the level of industrial adjustments.

(b) Intensifying competitiveness in US industry
The dramatic decline in the value of the dollar has spurred a strong recovery in the competitiveness of US exports. However, in order for the US to boost further exports to improve its trade balance, it must find its own ways to raise substantially the international competitiveness of its industry.

Japan, too, is obliged to cooperate in reviving American competitiveness by making direct investments through package transfers of capital and technology.

(c) Building a new international division of labor
In the past, the United States and Central and South American nations were very closely related trade partners. Recently, however, the United States and its Latin American partners have all become debtor nations. By contrast, Japan and the Asian NICs (Newly Industrialized Countries) maintain the world's highest economic growth rates and are expected to serve as a growth pole in the future.

The United States and the Latin American nations will not be able to reverse their debtor-nation status without building a new international division of labor in which Japan, the Asian NICs and Western European countries create a market for US and Latin American exports.

(d) Formation of a global finance order
During the course of correcting economic imbalances in the United States
and reducing the cumulative debt of developing nations, care must be
taken to avoid abrupt fluctuations in financal markets, such as currency
markets and interest rates, or a decline in living standards in debtor
nations. To avoid these problems, there must be a smooth infusion of
capital from the capital-surplus nations to the United States and developing countries. The public sector must lay the groundwork for such
infusion by taking measures to enhance its risk-compensation functions
and by working to stabilize currency fluctuations so as to reduce the risk
of exchange-rate volatility.

(e) Other possible scenarios for correcting the imbalance
Other possible scenarios for correcting global economic imbalances
might include encouraging the service trade to take greater advantage of
America's clear superiority in industries related to the intellectual property field. However, if conditions worsen, such a strategy would pose a
grave danger to the global economic order and might lead to a system of
government-controlled trade. The important point in any case is that
correcting the current imbalances must be done in a smooth manner that
will not threaten the existence of our global economic order founded on
free trade.

(3) The new industrial revolution

Innovative technological progress tends to empower rapid economic
development, as seen during the first pivotal technological revolution
based on the steam engine and coal- and steel-related technologies, and
also during the second technological revolution based on electricity and
telecommunications, automotive technology, the internal combustion
engine, and petroleum technologies. Today, new technological revolutions are already under way, this time centered on microelectronics, new
materials and biotechnology.

For example, progress in microelectronic technology at the atomic and
molecular level will not end with improvements in the integration,
reliability and speed of individual electronic products, but will extend to
the point where it has a major impact on education and culture through
the creation of information-processing systems that are more and more
sophisticated.

For new materials such as higher-temperature superconductors, progress in atomic-level control techniques for high polymers, new metals,
fine ceramics and other areas is yielding revolutionary discoveries and
has precipitated the germination of many future technological
innovations.

Biotechnology's rapid advances have revolutionized certain industrial technologies, and its elucidation of biological functions has produced a variety of technological spinoffs. Moreover, the hybrid technologies developed by biotechnology researchers have also resulted in remarkable spinoff effects that will benefit other industrial fields such as chemistry, foods, textiles and pharmaceuticals.

Engineering advances at the atomic and molecular levels, the trend toward a closer and more harmonious relationship between science and engineering, and the additional impetus to progress provided by hybrid technologies have together helped explode our traditional and relatively stable technological framework based on steel, chemistry, machinery, electronics, electricity and textiles – a framework under which we have lived since the second industrial revolution. Today's technological innovation is now reaching the stage where we can envision a new technological framework and the types of new viable industries it will include.

Today's technological breakthroughs are producing reforms in our production and management methods, and are giving rise to a variety of new products and new industries. This trend requires that businesses respond to consumer needs that reflect changing lifestyles and cultural styles so as to offer new cultural concepts regarding the use of psychologically appealing designs, fashions and merchandise.

For example, now that more people are experiencing material satisfaction and living longer lives, their concerns are turning toward health. Therefore, biotechnology companies are developing new medicines, and other companies are carrying forth medical and therapeutic technologies such as microelectronic robot assistants for the elderly, and are thereby preparing supply-side conditions responsive to the changing basic needs of the people.

The ongoing diffusion of audiovisual equipment based on microelectronics is expected to make a large contribution to the material affluence of people living today. In addition, advances in intelligent technology will enable the formation of information networks, including households, and offer a broad spectrum of information media, giving the general population access to a huge volume of information and a wide range of selections.

This progress in intelligent technology will also enable companies promptly to grasp the distribution level of consumer needs which are changing in line with diversifying demand, individualistic tastes, greater sophistication, and internationalization. Vertical coordination among upstream, midstream and downstream stages in the design-production-distribution process will enhance the efficiency of the supply system and help create and provide styles better attuned to prevailing attitudes and sensibilities.

In other words, the seeds planted by technological progress and the needs created by changes in our social structure will together fuel the growth of new markets and will help bring about renewed economic development.

From the long-term perspective, how we respond to this new industrial revolution will be the key to future economic development. Although this revolution is looked upon as a new source of energy to revitalize the global economy, such renewed growth may well cause serious problems for the many developing nations that may remain locked into the old technological framework.

It is therefore essential that the advanced nations construct a framework with the purpose of transferring new technologies – including those that involve issues relating to intellectual property rights – to enable global dispersion of the fruits produced by technological innovation and the new industrial revolution (see Table 2.3).

Table 2.3 The technological framework of the third technological revolution

Field of innovation	Today	Tomorrow
Microelectronics Elements	Semiconductors, ICs, LSIs, VLSIs	Molecular elements, quantization elements*
	Personal computers	Voice and image recognition devices Parallel processing mainframe computers
	Distributed processing systems	(Distributed processing systems) Neurocomputers†
	Expert systems	(Expert system)
	Fifth generation computers	(Fifth generation computers) Optical computers
	NMR-CT	Geological scanners

Systems	Robots, NC machine tools, FMS	Intelligent robots‡
	Submicron-order machining accuracy	Nanometer-order machining accuracy
New materials Materials	Superconductors	Room-temperature superconductors†
Energy	Atomic power	Nuclear fusion
	Jet engines	Ceramic engines
Biotechnology Chemistry, etc.	Bioreactor-based production	Breakthrough in biochemical processes† Protein engineering*
Medicine	Biotechnology-based production of pharmaceuticals	Genetic analysis
Agriculture	Hybridization	Breeding by gene recombination
Others		Biochips‡

* Example of atomic or molecular level control technology
† Example of meeting of science and engineering
‡ Example of hybrid technology.

2. Japan's role in the new globalism

(1) Downfall of the Pax Americana and the search for a new framework

The term 'Pax Americana' was coined to describe the relative order and peace that existed in the world following the Second World War and America's dominant economic, political and military power that provided the main support for such conditions. During this era, the global economic order was founded on free trade as spelled out under the GATT and a currency system that was firmly centered on the American dollar.

As discussed in the first section of this chapter, however, the global economic order, which is still basically defined within the framework of Pax Americana, is undergoing major conflict as the steadily weakening US economy's relative position on the global scale has provided the underpinnings for growing disequilibrium in balance of payments, wild fluctuations in currency exchange rates, and troubling signs of protectionism.

Amid this situation, Japan and West Germany consistently maintained capital surpluses and achieved creditor-nation status during the 1970s, ultimately becoming the world's largest creditor nations in 1985.

In the currency market, depreciation of the US dollar's value and correlative appreciation in the value of the Japanese yen and West German mark caused a corresponding shift in each of these currencies' position as an international currency, which led to an increase in Japan's and West Germany's relative economic weight in the global economy.

NEW GLOBAL ORDER

Looking toward the future of the global economy as we approach the twenty-first century, the world needs to find a new global order that replaces the outmoded Pax Americana. During this search, the following points should be considered.

First, it is essential that we avoid the pitfalls of the protectionism and regionalism that have been raising their ugly heads in recent years, and instead maintain a foundation of globalism.

Second, to ensure the survial of globalism, we must facilitate the revitalization of the US economy and industry, and thereby help revive and maintain the support the United States gives to globalism. At present, no other country can fill the position the United States holds to provide for international cooperation on all fronts, including politics and diplomacy.

Thirdly, the United States is no longer readily able to provide international economic cooperation on its own, and therefore it behoves Japan and the Western European countries also to provide support for the global economic system.

In today's global economic system, the relationship between politics and military affairs on one side, and economics and culture on the other, is clearly changing. However, Japan is not yet ready to take the place of the United States in any of these matters, and must instead stay with the Western European countries as a supporter of the United States.

Fourth and last, the dynamism exhibited by economies in the Asia/ Pacific region is being looked on as a support for the revitalization of the economy and industry of the United States.

DIFFICULTIES INVOLVED

Numerous difficulties will likely accompany the search for a new global economic order.

While pursuing the concept that Japan should extend more and more economic cooperation to the United States, care must be taken to ensure that Japan does not eventually undermine America's leadership in providing international economic cooperation, since such a trend could well fan the flames of jealous antagonism in the United States, provoke suspicion in Western Europe, and produce other international repercussions as Japan becomes perceived as an economic superpower.

With regard to the expanding cooperation with the Asia/Pacific nations, consideration must be given to the scenarios in which either Japan or the United States could become economically isolated. The dispelling of fears among Western European and Third World nations is also very important.

(2) Japan's role in the new globalism

In addition to affirming what has just been suggested concerning the new global economic order, Japan must work to emphasize and develop a new globalism that will rebuild the crisis-ridden one of today.

Building on the changing relationship in the world economic system between politics and the military on the one hand, and economics and culture on the other, the promotion of free and open economic and cultural exchanges will make for a healthier climate of international politics. Viewing their recognized value as facilitating global stability and progress, such exchanges will surely be oriented toward the formation of international solidarity centered on economics and culture.

Second, to enhance the effectiveness of the system of international organizations such as the GATT, the OECD, and the IMF, Japan must strive to empower them (by promoting GATT's Uruguay Round, for example) to create a multidimensional and open alignment of international relations that can function as a subsystem supporting multilateralism.

Specifically, we must work to strengthen economic and industrial cooperation between the United States and Japan to help maintain and restore the stabilizing influence of the United States on the global economic order (US–Japan link).

We must also strive toward the formation of a new international division of labor based on the circum-pan-Pacific (the US–Japan–Asia/ Pacific link), maintain the trilateral open system among Japan, the United States, and Western Europe (US–Japan–Western Europe link), and help build new cooperative relations between Latin America, Middle Eastern and African nations and the advanced industrialized countries.

Here, it is vital that these various links be open to erstwhile non-participating nations as well. Using these multi-layered open international relations as a subsystem, we must rebuild a global liberal economic system on top of it.

Naturally, when Japan participates in this subsystem and attempts to build new and harmonious relations with other nations or regions, Japan must remember not only where those nations or regions stand in relation to itself but also where it stands in relation to them. (See Appendix 4: Issues in various regions of the world and Japan's responses; Appendix 5: Japan as seen by the world.)

In developing stratified yet open relations of interdependency with the various other regions of the world, Japan must keep its eye on building a new global economic order that is different from US-oriented bilateralism or minilateralism. Although Japan, the United States and Western Europe will play a major role in supporting the global economic order, they should strive to shift the equilibrium of this support by enlisting the participation of the Asia/Pacific countries.

There is a need to avoid applying the rules of the advanced industrialized nations across the board and instead devise flexible international rules that account for the diverse stages of kinds of development among the world's nations. To be truly functional, the new globalism must be able to establish a framework that is liberal and generous enough to accommodate the views of various countries.

The final point is that, as a supporter of the new globalism, Japan must take the initiative in self-reform in order thoroughly to open itself up to other countries. Until now, Japan has pursued a lopsided internationalism that stresses only the outflow of finance, capital, people and companies to other countries. Now Japan needs to make this a two-way street by also promoting an inflow of goods and people from overseas.

More specifically, this means making Japan a major importer by further opening its markets and expanding imports of manufactured goods, and by becoming more enthusiastically open to participation and cultural exchanges involving visitors from foreign companies. In pursuing these activities, Japan will also be obliged to aid the correction of imbalances in the global economy. (See Appendix 6: Flow and fluctuation of trade among major nations.)

Finally, in view of the principle of openness in science and technology, Japan must present and implement new rules concerning intellectual property rights in order to facilitate the invigorating effects of technological and industrial innovations on the global economy.

3. US–Japan economic and industrial cooperation

(1) Outlook for the US economy and industrial competitiveness

COMPETITIVE RECOVERY

Although it is common knowledge that the competitiveness of US industry has been substantially weakened since the early 1980s, exports have recently been showing an increase (see Table 2.4). For example, in 1987 US exports increased by 11.5 per cent compared with the previous year, with machinery and transport-related equipment in particular showing marked strength. Impressive export surges have also been seen in office equipment, electrical machinery and aircraft (see Figure 2.2).

Table 2.4 US exports, 1983–7 (US$bn.)

1983	205.6
1984	224.0
1985	218.8
1986	226.8
1987	252.9
1st Quarter	57.9
2nd Quarter	62.4
3rd Quarter	62.2
4th Quarter	70.4

Source: statistics from US Department of Commerce.

Furthermore, the US dollar-based unit labor cost has also shown an improvement compared with that of Japan and West Germany. This has resulted in a corresponding degree of recovery in American industrial competitiveness, with an industrial facilities utilization rate that has almost reached the all-time high of 81 per cent. Meanwhile, the latest facility investment figure shows a large expansion in rationalization-related investments such as information-processing systems. However, not much of an increase has been observed in capacity-boosting investments related to direct production volume expansion. Consequently, in view of the fact that the United State is not experiencing a rise in surplus domestic production capacity, it must begin to devise microeconomic measures to boost production capacity in preparation for future export growth.

HIGH GROWTH POTENTIAL

Over the mid- to long-term future, US industry has several types of high growth potential internationally.

First, the US technological level is still far above that of other countries, including Japan, in both large-scale engineering fields, such aerospace, marine and resource-based energy, and in basic technology fields such as bioengineering, new materials and intelligence processing (see Figure 2.4).

The overwhelming superiority of the United States in science and technology is supported by its accumulation of a 'technological stockpile' or database environment, the quantity of its published research reports and the number of its technological patents sold to other countries. This stockpile is likely to last over the mid- to long-term future.

A second aspect of the high-growth potential of the United States is the enormous scale of its market, one which will continue to be affluent and pioneering in its demand structure even in comparison with other advanced industrialized nations.

Third, the United States is an advanced service-intensive nation in which the service industry claims about 70 per cent of the national income at factor cost. Moreover, its service industry has paramount superiority internationally.

In 1986, the US service trade balance (defined as the invisible trade balance minus the investment earnings balance) showed a surplus of about US$2.6 billion. Furthermore, excluding travel and transport services and counting only revenues from patent royalties and from service fees collected in banking, insurance, advertising and accounting services, while Japan and West Germany both recorded deficits in these areas, the United States chalked up a surplus of about US$12.5 billion.

In terms of productivity in the service sector, the United States stands head and shoulders above Japan in all areas.

When one surveys the service industry, it is clear that there are several reasons why it is likely that the United States will maintain the dominant international competitiveness of its service sector. The US service industry is developing a global management strategy, has accumulated a wealth of expertise, has strong product development skills and powerful technological capacity for making clerical work more systematic and efficient and is well into the intelligent age with investments in computers and strength in software development.

Figure 2.2 US Export recovery by category

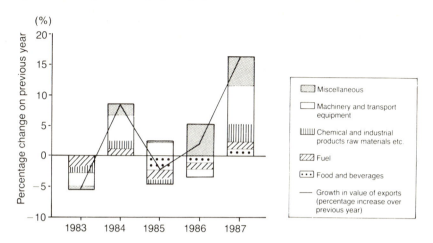

Source: statistics from US Department of Commerce.

Figure 2.3 dollar-based unit labor costs in the united states, japan and west germany, 1960-86

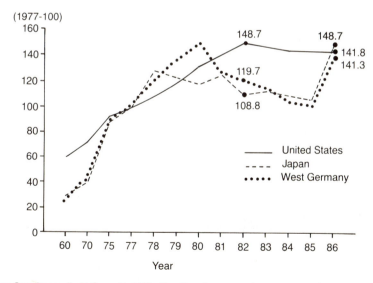

Notes: See Appendix 7: Capacity Utilization Trends among Japanese and American manufactures; and Appendix 8: Plant Investment in the United States and Japan.
   Each country's figure is set at 100 in the base year 1977; unit labor cost is equal to real wages divided by real labor productivity.

Source: Monthly Labor Review, US Department of Commerce.

The following comparisons of American and Japanese technology levels in various fields are taken from the results of surveys conducted between 1982 and 1984 by Japan's Agency of Industrial Science and Technology and by the Japan Techno-Economics Society (JATES). More details are found in Appendix 35.

In what field is each nation strongest?
The United States excels in seminal technological fields such as large-scale technologies and basic technologies. Japan excels in technologies related to consumer needs such as public welfare and production technologies.

Types of seminal technological fields in which the United States is superior
Large-scale engineering fields
Japan has surpassed the United States in certain areas of large-scale engineering such as aerospace, marine technologies, nuclear engineering and resource and energy development, in general, as well as other highly technical fields. These areas include material engineering, light water reactor manufacturing and safety engineering. However, Japan still lags behind in the more general large-scale engineering applications such as space stations, satellite delivery and recovery, nuclear fusion, radioactive waste processing, coal and gas liquefaction, resource exploration and ultra low- and high-pressure applications.

Basic technologies
Japan has caught up with the United States in basic technology fields such as bioengineering, new materials and basic intelligent-processing technologies as well as in technologies related to the production of mainframe computers. The United States, however, still enjoys an overall advantage in areas such as recombinant genetics, artificial intelligence (AI) and database development.

Fields in which the United States maintains a near monopoly on the market and has a strong lead in seminal research
In fields like civilian aircraft, medical and social welfare technologies and environmental monitoring, Japan has accumulated a wealth of relevant technologies such as with development of artificial hearts and urban disaster prevention. But in general, these types of research begin in Japan several years after originating in the United States. The gap between the two countries here is not decreasing.

Types of market-oriented technological fields (geared to consumer needs) in which Japan is superior
Development of products for the general public
Japan is clearly ahead in production and product-development engineering related to electronics products used by the general consumer, office equipment and other machinery that is widely available via retail outlets. Specifically, Japan was the first to succeed in the commercial development of such products as household VCRs, video disks and facsimile machines.

Production engineering
Japan and the United States each have their own relative strengths and weaknesses in areas such as ceramics production for electronic engineering, semiconductor fabrication technologies, IC memory chip manufacturing technologies and LSI inspection technologies. Japan generally lags behind in design, materials, refining and precision control technologies and leads in reliability testing and automation technologies. If we also take into account Japan's dominance in production-level management such as in process management and quality control techniques, we can conclude that Japan enjoys an overall superiority in production engineering.

Engineering fields that require large-scale funding
Japan has achieved a very high level of technology in traffic control systems, public telecommunications infrastructure, dam construction and other engineering fields that require large-scale funding. Japan particularly excels in areas such as magnetically levitated (maglev) trains and large-scale residential construction.

Fields where the United States and Japan are roughly equal
The United States and Japan are running neck-and-neck in the area of industrial machinery such as industrial robots, machining centers and machine tools. Specifically, Japan leads in control technologies, while the United States has the edge in design, adaptive control and ultra-precision machine tools.

Figure 2.4 Technology levels in the United States and Japan

PROBLEMS

However, there are also several problems regarding the mid- to long-term recovery of US industrial competitiveness. The first is the weakening trend in the US domestic base of R & D and production facilities due to an expansion in overseas direct investment that has moved many of these facilities overseas. As a result, the United States has recently been developing a growing import dependence on capital goods and consumer durables such as machine tools and electronic equipment. This trend can only work to restrict future US economic growth, both quantitatively and qualitatively. (See Appendix 9: Product categories in US trade balance.)

Even though the United States enjoys clear superiority in basic technological fields, its inferiority to Japan in production engineering, which includes management at the commercial development and production stages, means the US industry has lost its international competitiveness in product markets.

And finally, American companies need to deal with various general management issues, while manufacturing companies are confronted with problems in human resource development and job assignments. Some of the more characteristic issues are described below.

(i)   Due to a management emphasis on short-term gains and an outbreak of 'merger and acquisition fever,' companies generally do not pursue projects requiring stable, long-term efforts, such as the development of new products and technologies, plant investment and construction of sales networks.

(ii)   Very few companies are export-oriented because the traditional market for US companies is domestic.

(iii) Management and labor practices are such that they do not let workers fully exhibit their abilities.

(iv)   The most talented engineers and managers do not work at manufacturing companies. It is especially true that high-quality engineers tend not to work in the production division of factories, which explains why US production engineering lags conspicuously and product reliability does not improve. Instead, the better engineers can be found in the sectors of basic research and defense.

FUTURE REVITALIZATION

The rate at which the United States is currently reducing its balance of payments deficit is not enough to put the nation squarely on the road toward becoming a creditor nation again. When this fact is considered in conjunction with the other mid- and long-term problems outlined above, it becomes clear that the revitalization of the US economy and industry will not be easy.

(2) Japan's response in seeking the revitalization of the US economy and industry

Japan must work toward helping to lay the foundations for a new global economic order by lending cooperation to the revitalization of the US economy and industry. There are a number of ways this can be accomplished.

Stronger policy coordination

Policy coordination must be established in macroeconomic and semi-macroeconomic areas such as industrial restructuring.

The smooth implementation of structural adjustments in US industry aimed at solid improvement in competitiveness must be clearly based upon stability in domestic commodity prices and currency exchange rates. To bring about such stability, the currency and macroeconomic policies of Japan, the United States and other major advanced industrialized nations must be coordinated to a much greater degree than seen thus far.

In addition to its energetic efforts toward industrial restructuring, the United States will need to adopt semi-macro and microeconomic policies such as the promotion of investments that will bring new strength to its industrial competitiveness. On the other hand, Japan is expected to change from an export-oriented, import-conservative nation to a more domestic-demanding, active import nation, in terms of industrial structural adjustment. Thus, in order to restore the competitiveness of the US economy and industry and smoothly solve the trade imbalance, both Japan and the United States should cooperate not only in macroeconomic policies but also in semi-microeconomic policies including industrial reform.

From this perspective, it becomes apparent that such restructuring efforts between Japan and the United States should include not only government-based efforts but also a continually interactive program involving researchers and industrialists (such as a Wise Men's group on industrial restructuring). Such a group would be able to find areas in which their policies could be coordinated and could contribute much to the revitalization of the US economy and industry by translating Japan's own experiences in restructuring its industries into the context of US industrial restructuring.

The joining together of Japanese and US industries

Conditions such as worsening US–Japan trade friction and the strong yen have spurred Japanese companies in fields such as electrical machinery and general machinery to establish factories overseas. In addition, Japanese and US companies have rapidly broadened the scope of their joint efforts in various kinds of tie-ups including joint R & D projects, OEM contracts, and purchases of imported parts and semi-finished products.

This type of broadened interdependence between Japanese and American industries, centered on direct investments from Japan, can be seen as a joining together of the industries of the two countries. The growing interdependence usually involves transfers to US companies of Japan's superior production technologies, as well as management techniques relating to production, inventory management and sales, which tend to foster improved labor relations and stronger competitiveness within the domestic market. Such a trend is sure to contribute substantially to improving US industrial and export strength.

This coming together of Japanese and US industries will usher in a new global division of labor and a greater flow of technology and knowledge, which is quite likely to help strengthen mutual understanding and alleviate opposition based on each nation's relative advantages and disadvantages.

In view of the above, it is clear that the promotion of enhanced cooperation between Japan and the United States is vitally important for both the revitalization of US industry and the internationalization of Japanese companies.

For Japan's part, efforts toward thoroughly opening the Japanese market and expanding product imports will help provide an export market for US industry. These efforts are, therefore, an essential part of Japan's cooperation in aiding the revitalization of US industry.

APPROACHES TO THE CONCEPT OF JAPANESE–AMERICAN FREE TRADE

Given the apparent broadening of economic interdependence between Japan and the United States, one could argue that the two countries are now obliged to build a new institutional framework – a 'new free-trade pact' – which, among other things, would call for a bilateral effort toward developing the economies of both nations.

This would offer definite advantages: through promoting liberal competition, it would help revitalize; it would support the pro-free-trade stance and oppose protectionism; and in the medium to long run, it would help to avoid useless economic friction once a new framework for comprehensive negotiations is established.

On the other hand, there would also be some disadvantages. For example, it would exacerbate fears that Japan's export dependence on the United States would grow or that such a plan would have a profound impact on certain industrial sectors in each country.

It could also be argued that opening such a bilateral free trade pact with other nations would further help to maintain and strengthen the free-trade system. While this is true, it also stands to reason that since Japan and the United States together account for such a large portion of the global economy, their solidarity alone would be enough to influence third-party nations. In this case, however, since stimulating the growth potential of the Asia/Pacific region is essential for the healthy development of the global economy, it is important to look at US–Japan cooperative relations within the context of broader cooperative relations among Japan, the United States and the Asia/Pacific region.

JAPAN'S ADVOCACY OF HEALTHY US–JAPAN RELATIONS

The major prerequisite for revitalization of the US economy and industry is self-help efforts on the part of the United States itself. That is why Japan must strongly suggest to the United States that it enact a forceful and sustained curtailment of its budget deficit – the leading cause of the trade deficit – and take strong action to beef up its industrial competitiveness.

Recently, Americans have come to feel strongly that 'unfair trade practices' on the part of US major trading partners are the primary reason why the trade imbalance is not being corrected. This argument could lead to the erroneous conclusion that these trading partners are being unilaterally unfair. Moreover, after a heating-up of American–Japanese competition in high-technology fields, the US opted to invoke the 'national defense clauses' of legislation such as Section 232 of the Trade Expansion Act of 1962. Such defense clauses have vague spheres of application, and by applying them very broadly, industrial interests in the United States have been able to go beyond the traditional interpretation of such clauses as 'national security safegards' to apply them instead of protectionist measures.

Such conclusions of unfairness based purely on US standards of fairness and such broad interpretation of defense clauses have gone hand in hand with US advocacy of 'sectorial reciprocity,' which seeks to ensure balanced trade in certain specified industrial sectors. This policy of 'sectorial reciprocity' is in fact just another form of protectionism and it inevitably leads to retaliatory measures against trading partners. This protectionist trend not only works directly against efforts toward greater competitiveness and export strength in US industry but, ironically, also works to undermine the system of free trade that the United States itself built following the end of the Second World War.

For its part, Japan, still hoping to build sound relations with the United States, is pointing out the problems inherent in the unilateral argument of unfairness and the protectionist measures being advocated in the United States. As an alternative, Japan is pushing for corrections in bilateral trade to be worked out within a multilateral system such as GATT.

4. Development cooperation in the Asia/Pacific region

(1) Development possibilities and destabilizing factors in the Asia/Pacific region

DEVELOPMENT POSSIBILITIES

The economies of the Asia/Pacific region continue to have a generally high rate of growth, especially among the Asian NICs. Looking at the average real GDP growth figures for the first half of the 1980s, we see that while the advanced industrialized countries averaged 2.3 per cent growth, the Asian NIC economies grew at about three times that (6.7 per cent). Even the ASEAN countries, including those which had suffered from depressed prices for primary products, managed to average 2.7 per cent (excluding Singapore and Brunei).

This high growth among economies in the Asia/Pacific region has been seen as a remarkably good performance amidst a global economy that was undergoing structural changes. Also, in comparison with the economies of advanced industrialized countries at the time, the Asia/Pacific economies appeared particularly healthy. The economies of countries in the Asia/Pacific region are expected to maintain similar high levels of growth in the future. (See Appendix 10: Population, GNP and economic growth in the Asia/Pacific region.)

INHERENT DESTABILIZING FACTORS

Despite their high growth, the Asia/Pacific economies are faced with a number of destabilizing factors.

(a) Fears of protectionist power in the United States
The US foreign trade imbalance has clearly taken a turn for the better but still remains at a very high level. There are fears that the United States may turn to protectionism as a means of rectifying the imbalance. These trends run the risk of shrinking foreign trade, thereby putting a damper on economic growth in the Asia/Pacific region.

(b) Deflationary effects of correcting the US deficit
The process of curtailing the US twin deficit (or triple deficit if we include the net savings deficit in the private sector) will inevitably lead to a slowdown in the American economy. When this happens, the United States can no longer be expected to absorb as many imports. This market shrinkage will tend to restrict the growth of the Asia/Pacific countries that generally depend on the United States to provide a large market for their exports.

1: The United States decided on 29 January 1988, effective as of 2 January 1989, to cease granting preferential customs treatment to four Asian NICs.

2: The EC decided effective 1 January 1988 to cease granting preferential customs treatment to South Korea, as part of a discriminatory measure to protect intellectual property rights.

3: Exchange rate adjustments and requests for market liberalization have been demanded of the NICs by the conference of finance ministers and central bank governors from seven leading advanced industrialized nations (the G7) as well as others.

Figure 2.5 Recent measures taken with regard to the Asian NICs.

(c) Inherent weaknesses in Asian NICs

The economies of the Asian NICs, which have had the highest sustained growth among nations in the Asia/Pacific region, are nonetheless beset with the following inherent weaknesses:

(i)   The Asian NICs have a very high export dependency (59 per cent on average, compared with a 14 per cent average among advanced industrialized nations) and therefore their economic structures are easily affected by global economic trends.

(ii)   The Asian NICs lag behind in developing supporting industries to brace comprehensively economic development from the foundation up. In Taiwan, although medium-sized and small companies are developing, especially in light industries, the country is behind in long-term technological development and plant investment.

(iii) City states such as Hong Kong and Singapore have very limited domestic demand due to their small populations (six million in Hong Kong in 1986 and three million in Singapore), and therefore they are necessarily export-dependent economies. Since both Hong Kong and Singapore trade primarily in manufactured goods, they must also import in great quantities. Hong Kong has maintained an approximate balance of trade while in 1987 Singapore recorded a trade deficit of nearly US$4 billion.

In view of these inherent weaknesses in the economies of the Asian NICs, if the advanced industrialized nations begin to perceive increased exports from the Asian NICs as a threat, it can only have an adverse effect on the development of these countries, which is regarded as a springboard for the future development of the global economy. (See Figure 2.5 and Appendix 11: Trade structure of the Asian NICs.)

(d) Dependence on primary goods production

The ASEAN countries and Australia have always had economic structures that are generally dependent on the production of primary goods.

The major reason for the recent problems in the economies of primary-goods producers such as Indonesia is thought to be the lower prices for such primary goods as crude oil. The outlook is that international market conditions for primary products are likely to continue hindering the economic growth of such countries.

Although industrialization is progressing rapidly in some ASEAN countries such as Thailand, it will take quite some time for industrialized growth to be achieved throughout the Asia/Pacific region.

To attain stable development and contribute to the development and vitality of the global economy in the future, nations in the Asia/Pacific region must make the most of their growth potential and must mutually cooperate to rid themselves of the destabilizing factors described above.

(2) The need for development cooperation from Japan

Japan should do everything it can actively to promote development cooperation in the Asia/Pacific region. The promotion of the Asia/Pacific region's growth potential and dynamism is essential for stimulating the global economy and correcting its imbalances, and because the success of the Asia/Pacific countries in overcoming the destabilizing factors described above to achieve solid economic growth is important for ensuring political stability in the region. Specifically, Japan should take note of the points listed below.

(i)   The diversity of the Asia/Pacific region must be respected. The Asia/Pacific region includes advanced industrialized countries, NICs and developing countries. In other words, it is a mixture of countries that have reached different stages of economic development. Moreover, these nations are also diverse in terms of race, culture and religion. This diversity in itself is a source of the region's vitality. Any cooperation pursued in this region must respect its multifarious character.

(ii) Cooperative relations must be built realistically and moderately. Cooperation must be pursued in a realistic and moderate manner that is in line with the diversity of the Asia/Pacific region.

(iii) Cooperation must be in accord with the development stage of each nation. In contrast with cooperation among advanced industrialized nations such as the EC nations, which is based simply on reciprocity, cooperation with Asian NICs, ASEAN countries and other Asia/Pacific countries must take into consideration each country's stage of development. Furthermore, it is vital that such cooperation lead to the encouragement of each country's self-motivated participation in international economic activity in a manner suited to its stage of development.

(iv) Economic strength must be maintained to avoid increased debt problems. Debt problems must not be allowed to rob the Asia/Pacific region of its dynamism, especially since this dynamism is expected to be a key propellant for the future development of the global economy. Even among the developing nations in this region, it is important that they commit themselves to sustained self-help efforts to ensure sound economic growth.

(v) Cooperative relations must be of an open nature. If, despite efforts to develop cooperation in the Asia/Pacific region, these countries fall into the trap of pursuing protectionist or regionalist policies, such policies would invite a shrinkage of world trade and eventually backfire as they restrict the possibilities for economic development of the countries in this region. Consequently, the Asia/Pacific region needs to pursue cooperative relations that are open to countries in other regions.

(3) Japan's role and response

In seeking to strengthen cooperative relations in the Asia/Pacific region, Japan should pursue the following measures and thereby help build a new international division of labor. In doing so, Japan must work to build cooperative relations that recognize the particular characteristics of each nation or area in the Asia/Pacific region, such as the highly export-dependent Asian NICs, the rapidly industrializing ASEAN countries, the nations of Oceania that depend so profoundly on exports of primary goods and natural resources, and finally China, a nation that is energetically pursuing a policy of openness and economic reform.

TRADE MEASURES: MAKING JAPAN A MAJOR IMPORTER

In the future, trade relations among the United States, Japan and the rest of Asia will require a reduction of the US trade deficit (i.e. putting a damper on the growth of US imports and decreasing the amount of US-bound exports from Asia) and at the same time sufficient growth in Asian exports to meet the needs of Asian economic development. To achieve both of these seemingly contradictory goals, Japan must gradually increase its imports of Asian products and become one of the world's major product importers. This expansion of imports by Japan will enable the Asian exporters to correct their lopsided dependence on the US market and promote their sound economic development.

Once these Asian nations reach a certain point in their economic development, they can themselves become markets for other exporters. In fact, US exports to Asian NICs showed a threefold increase last year. Japan should look to this example as it prepares its domestic environ-

The so-called New AID Plan was first announced by the Japanese Minister of International Trade and Industry, Hajime Tamura, during his January 1987 visit to Bangkok. Briefly, the plan calls for Japan to work toward providing comprehensive cooperation to various Asian nations in a manner that suits their particular circumstances and that reflects the Asian developing countries' most recent economic cooperation needs. Such considerations include the need for support in cultivating industries that will attract foreign investment from mainly private-sector sources.

In concrete terms, Japan will need to devise cooperation policies that select appropriate industries for each of the developing nations and that include specific industry-cultivation plans. In addition, Japan must pursue a threefold implementation of this policy, including: the provision of capital and technological assistance for the cultivation of private-sector industrial divisions; the promotion of Japanese direct investments in these nations; and the provision of an expanding import market for industrial goods produced by these developing nations.

Figure 2.6 Summary of Japan's 'New AID Plan'

ment for such an expansion of two-way trade and work toward solid expansion of imports from other Asian nations.

INVESTMENT MEASURES: TOWARD A WELL-COORDINATED HORIZONTAL DIVISION OF LABOR

In the area of industrial support for trade relations, Japan must build upon its traditional relations based on a vertical division of labor between itself and the ASEAN nations by adding new relations based on a well-coordinated horizontal division of labor.

During the yen's recent steep climb, many of Japan's private-sector companies moved quickly to internationalize their operations and also joined US companies in developing an international division of labor that took advantage of market mechanisms and involved the Asia/Pacific region. In such undertakings, Japan must always be careful to make investments that will boost production capacity in a manner that supports demand.

ECONOMIC COOPERATION MEASURES: ENERGETIC PROMOTION OF A 'NEW AID PLAN'

In addition to cooperation in trade and investment, Japan must positively promote the extension of economic cooperation to developing countries in the Asia/Pacific region. In particular, Japan should provide comprehensive support for self-initiated economic development efforts by Asian developing countries by energetically developing a New Asian Industries Development (AID) Plan that will direct concentrated economic and technological cooperation to target areas (see Figure 2.6).

ENERGY COOPERATION MEASURES: PROMOTION OF ENERGY COOPERATION IN THE PACIFIC REGION

The Asia/Pacific region will continue to experience high growth in its energy demand. Most of the countries in the region, particularly the NICs, are very dependent on petroleum. Therefore, a stable supply of energy must be secured to maintain a foundation for the region's continued economic development.

Japan has already responded to this issue by inaugurating the Symposium on Pacific Energy Cooperation, promoting the concept of a trans-Pacific flow of coal and encouraging international energy cooperation projects such as those for electricity and new energy development. However, these cooperation projects must be carried forth in a smooth and steady manner.

PROMOTION OF GREATER INTERACTION

The Asia/Pacific region is a diverse region that includes not only advanced industrialized nations such as Japan, the United States, Canada and Australia but also the Asian NICs, various developing nations such as ASEAN nations, and even a socialist nation, China.

Although we may rightfully conclude that this diversity lends vitality to the region, it is equally true that such diversity has also made it difficult to build a foundation for smooth cooperation. Therefore, it is important to establish the means by which nations of this region can interact more freely and discuss the policy issues at hand, thereby furthering the cause of mutual understanding and cooperation.

In this situation, Japan has proposed that a new 'organization for cooperation' (tentative name) be established to promote cooperation within the Asia/Pacific region. However, implementing such a proposition will require a multifaceted and broad-ranging study of issues, including the need for establishing such an organization, its economic significance and the degree of interest of the related countries. At the same time, consideration would also need to be given to the opinions of third-party countries.

OTHER MEASURES

In addition to the measures just described, Japan must support the continued progress of cooperation projects already under way in the Asia/Pacific region, such as the creation of an international inter-industry relations table, an agreement among Pacific nations regarding cooperation in the exploration of deep-sea resources and the concept of a multifunctional policy.

Japan must also actively investigate possibilities for joint research projects concerning cooperation in the Asia/Pacific region.

5. Maintaining a base for industrial development through currency stabilization

(1) The need for currency stabilization

The postwar world currency system began under a fixed exchange rate system that was based on the value of gold or on the gold-linked US dollar (and included an adjustable peg which permitted changes in currency values to correct fundamental imbalances). This system continued until August 1971 when, in what Japan refers to as the 'Nixon Shock,' US President Richard Nixon put an end to gold/dollar convertibility. With the exception of the Smithsonian system which lasted from December 1971 to March 1973, the major industrialized nations' currencies have since fluctuated under a floating exchange rate system. Even during this era of floating exchange rates, the US dollar has been the most traded currency internationally and has functioned as the key exchange currency. In recent years, however, the exchange value of the dollar has fluctuated dramatically, which reflects the weakening of the US economy.

Considering that the role of finance is to fund actual economic activity, physical economy is really the main element and finance is no more than a lubricant to facilitate smooth functioning of the economy. In fact, however, wild fluctuations in currency exchange rates have created an environment in which plant and R & D investments face the risk of becoming unproductive, and companies have been obligated to respond accordingly. In addition, with exchange rates continually being divorced from economic fundamentals, a distorted allocation of resources between trade-related goods and non-trade-related goods has resulted. Such investment risks and warped resource allocations are among the ill effects of unstable currency exchange rates. These adverse effects, moreover, can have a negative influence on the restructuring of the global economy. An example of this is the slowdown that has occurred in investments in the expansion of manufacturing capacity in the United States; insufficient investment has pushed the US capacity usage rate to over 80 per cent.

This is why the world currency system must be viewed as an international public property which cannot be left to market control alone. Instead, the costs of policy coordination must be borne proportionately by each country's government in order to increase the stability of the system. Considering that Japan was a beneficiary of the world currency system for a long time after the Second World War and that the continuing slide of the United States into debtor-nation status can only weaken its position within this system, Japan, as the world's largest creditor nation, is obliged to take on a larger and more appropriate proportion of this cost burden.

(2) Toward a stable international currency system

Major changes will inevitably need to be made as long as the current unbalanced global situation, including the large US balance of payments deficit (i.e. net foreign debts of the United States) and the accumulated debts of developing countries, persists, even if some kind of fixed-rate international currency system is introduced. Moreover, considering the policy coordination efforts that have been made thus far, Japan's response for the time being should be to work energetically to shape the world currency system by improving the functions of the existing floating exchange system by helping eliminate the global economic imbalance.

However, even if we view physical economy-oriented stimulation of industrial activity as the means for eliminating the global economic imbalance, devoted efforts must also be made concurrently toward stabilizing the currency system. Therefore, we must undertake a wide-ranging study aimed at the establishment of a stable international currency system, for example one which includes a reference zone for exchange rate fluctuations. It is also important to carry out the following three measures to lay the groundwork for policy coordination and simultaneously to address the needs for industrial revitalization, currency stabilization and elimination of global economic imbalances.

The first measure is to work toward building a system of policy coordination that is based on multifaceted surveillance of the principal objective economic indicators. The system will have to be broad enough to encompass not only easily coordinated policy areas, such as those of exchange-rate intervention and finance, but also fiscal (including tax), industrial and structural adjustment policies.

The second measure involves strengthening the system of coordinated intervention among monetary authorities by expanding the scope of swap trading, making greater use of special drawing rights and gradually narrowing down exchange-rate fluctuations that exceed permissible limits.

The third measure seeks to counter the turmoil in exchange rates which has been caused by the steady decline in confidence in the US dollar. This measure would encompass comprehensive dollar-bracing policies, such as issuing US bonds denominated in foreign currencies. (See Appendix 12: Evaluation of options for changing the world currency system.)

The first stage of the dollar crisis occurred during the shift to a floating exchange rate system following the August 1971 abolishment of the gold standard. These events had been precipitated by a decline in the international competitiveness of the United States, which became apparent in the worsening US trade deficit (US$2.6 billion in 1970 and US$2.3 billion in 1971).

The second stage came in 1977 and 1978 when the dollar fell below the Y200 level. This sudden decline was preceded by a skyrocketing surge in the US balance of payments deficit (from US$4.2 billion in 1976 to US$14.5 billion in 1977 and US$15.5 billion in 1978). The United States responded to this crisis by launching bold defensive measures that involved pumping US$30 billion – nearly double the 1978 foreign deficit – into currency markets as intervention capital and also as various discount-rate transactions.

The third stage was mainly characterized by the colossal blow dealt to confidence in the dollar by the soaring leap in the net US debt that had become well-established by 1986 (from US$3.6 billion at the end of 1984 to US$1.12 trillion one year later). This third stage can be broken down into the following three aspects.

The first involves the period following the 'Plaza Accord' of September 1985 when, after it became generally acknowledged that the overvalued dollar was the primary cause of external disequilibrium among the advanced industrialized nations, these nations sought to put downward pressure on the dollar. However, the dollar declined at a faster rate than had been intended by the various government authorities, dropping to the level of 160 yen to the dollar by July 1986. Behind this drastic shift are other fundamental macroeconomic changes, such as the worsening of the American private sector's savings-to-investment balance deficit (up from US$8.8 billion in 1986 to US$43.4 billion in 1987), and a steep drop in oil prices (London blend fell from US$25.55/barrel in late December 1985 to US$8.70/barrel in late July 1986).

The second aspect concerns the period following the 'Louvre Accord' of February 1987, when the emphasis was placed on stabilizing exchange rates, since it was generally agreed that exchange rate levels had moved to within a range that reflected economic fundamentals and that this shift had also helped correct external disequilibrium. This second aspect is also characterized by a further exacerbation of the US non-trade deficit (from US$1.4 billion surplus for the second quarter of 1987 to US$140 million deficit in the third) and the postponement of deliberations on fiscal deficit reduction, which led to doubts concerning the possibilities for correction of the external disequilibrium of the United States. This issue, along with other problems such as the standoff between the United States and West Germany on financial policies, formed the backdrop for the steep plunges in stock market prices that occurred in October 1987 and the ongoing rapid depreciation of the dollar.

The third aspect concerns what occurred in the wake of the December 1987 joint declaration (the 'Christmas Accord') of the G7 nations which had met to plan a restoration of the framework for cooperation that had been established by the 'Louvre Accord.' Although it was agreed that some progress had been made on correcting external disequilibrium, the G7 delegates sought to place an even greater emphasis on stabilizing the dollar with the hope of avoiding a recurrence of the confusion that prevailed in financial markets following shocks such as the recent stock market crashes (see Figure 2.8).

Figure 2.7 The dollar crisis

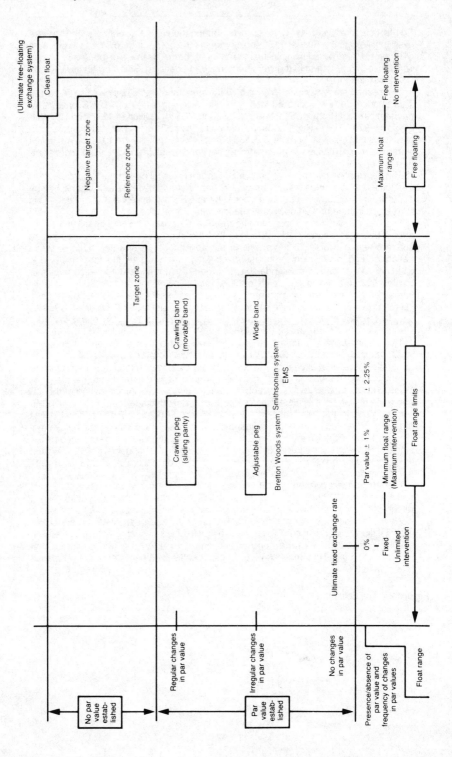

(3) Promoting the internationalization of the yen and of Japan's finance markets

As confidence in the dollar declines, the yen is gradually taking on a greater role as an international currency. With this period of internationalization of the yen, it is important to make it a more accessible currency by ensuring that non-Japanese resident investors are able to purchase and manage yen-based capital smoothly and economically. To this end, Japan must further open its markets to other countries, such as the South East Asian nations, while promoting yen-based trade transactions and looking into the establishment of a yen-based international commodities market.

To prepare for the yen's further internationalization, Japan needs to work toward expanding its short-term finance markets, primarily short-term treasury bonds and short-term government securities, which are both reliable and suitable for foreign currency reserves. Japan must also further promote the development of its international trade markets in Tokyo and other cities by liberalizing interest rates, alleviating restrictions on its domestic bond market and by opening its financial markets to overseas financial institutions. (See Appendix 13: Currency-specific distribution ratios of monetary authorities' foreign currency holdings.)

6. Expanding the international finance environment

(1) The importance of responding with actual economic measures

So far responses to the problem of accumulated debt have focused on finance-related measures (refinancing existing debts and securing development capital for the future) that have been needed to avoid an international finance crisis. However, the problem of accumulated debt cannot truly be resolved unless the debtor nations improve their own ability to repay their outstanding loans (i.e. their ability to bring in foreign currency) and thereby put themselves on the road to future self-sufficiency in economic development. Accordingly, what is needed to meet the debt problem are not just finance-related measures but also the application of procured capital toward improving the ability of the debtor nations to pull themselves out of debt, and this means actual economic measures such as restructuring the economy and cultivating industry.

The major prerequisite for such an economic response is self-help efforts on the part of the developing countries themselves, such as efforts to improve macroeconomic stability and to raise economic efficiency by relaxing domestic restrictions. For their part, the advanced industrialized nations should make use of the World Bank and other international institutions to provide comprehensive cooperation to these developing nations by combining capital and technical cooperation with direct investments in and expansion of imports from these nations, all in a manner which is appropriate to the circumstances of each particular developing nation.

Because the accumulated debt situation, economic conditions and political and cultural circumstances vary from one debtor nation to another, it is vital that these responses be flexible and versatile enough to suit the particular situation in each country. For example, among the world's poorest nations, such as certain sub-Saharan nations, nearly all of the foreign debts are owed to foreign governments and the amount of these outstanding debts is relatively small. An appropriate response in such cases would be for the advanced industrialized nations to make special accommodations such as relaxing their economic aid conditions (e.g. by raising their aid ceilings). As for nations such as the major debtor nations of Latin America, which have amassed large debts that are mainly owed to private banks, these nations generally have latent economic strength in terms of resources and industrial capabilities. The response to their problems, therefore, should be based on a plan to improve their loan repayment abilities by promoting mid- to long-term economic growth. Such a plan would need to have the consensus of the parties concerned and would also need to respect market mechanisms and make use of various financial measures to gradually reduce the outstanding debts of these countries in real terms (see Table 2.5).

Table 2.5 Debts among developing countries (US$bn.)

	1983	1984	1985	1986	1987	1988
Countries reporting to the World Bank	808	877	949	1,021	1,085	1,135
Long-term debts*	639	714	784	871	930	980
(Public-sector funding sources)	222	257	296	343	375	405
(Private-sector funding sources)	417	457	489	528	555	575
Short-term debts*	138	130	128	110	113	155
IMF credit*	30	33	38	40	42	
Other developing countries	86	81	87	99	105	110
Total	894	958	1,038	1,120	1,190	1,245

*1987 figures are actual results and 1988 figures are projections.
Source: 'World Debt Table (1987-88),' World Bank (see Appendix 14: Evaluation of response measures and proposals: Appendix 15: Principal debt indicators debtor nations: Appendix 16: Accumulated debts among developing countries).

(2) Japan's response

EXPANDING THE FLOW OF CAPITAL TO DEVELOPING COUNTRIES

The flow of capital from advanced industrialized nations to developing nations has decreased since 1981. Japan, as the world's largest supplier of capital, is expected to take the initiative in expanding its capital flow to developing nations. It has taken a firm first step in this direction by adopting measures to recycle over US$30 billion in capital over a three-year period. However, in addition to a thorough implementation of these measures, Japan must promote a much wider scope of mid- and long-range public- and private-sector capital flow to developing countries, including direct investments by the Japanese private sector. In so doing, these public- and private-sector funds must be targeted according to the particular needs of the recipient countries and should be arranged in an optimum capital recycling combination so as to yield the maximum benefits in fostering the economic development of these countries.

(a) Expansion of official development assistance
The developing countries that are suffering from large accumulated debts are in desperate need of capital at favorable terms. Although Japan has the world's second-largest official development assistance (ODA) budget, these ODA funds correspond to only 0.29 per cent of Japan's GNP, which is below the 0.35 per cent average ODA/GNP ratio among member nations of the OECD's Development Assistance Committee. In fact, Japan ranks fifteenth among the eighteen DAC member nations in this regard. Japan must do its utmost to boost the quantity and enhance the quality (i.e. to provide easy terms) of its ODA to reflect its current position in the world. (See Appendix 17: Economic cooperation record; Appendix 18: Comparison of ODA results among DAC nations, 1986; and Appendix 19: The structure of trade insurance.)

(b) Recycling private-sector capital
To increase its flow of capital to developing countries, Japan should emphasize such capital recycling methods as overseas investment of its abundant private-sector surplus and new extensions of credit. Such methods generally involve the transfer of such resources as equipment, technology and management expertise, which are essential for industrial development, and can be expected directly to aid economic development in the recipient countries. Moreover, such direct investment provides capital that is free of loan obligations and thus does not add to the repayment burden of the recipient country. These countries, therefore, tend to regard this type of capital flow as very desirable. However, since the private sector demands a relatively high return on its investments, any boost in private-sector capital flow into regions plagued by worsen-

ing accumulated debt problems will have to be preceded by the following types of public-sector measures, which are intended to support the efforts of recipient countries in preparing a viable investment environment.

(i) Expansion of trade insurance to cover investment risks. The exacerbation of the accumulated debt problem means that general risks such as those involving foreign currency transfer and a high degree of political instability can now be found in most large debtor nations. The private sector cannot be expected to bear this kind of burden on its own and will therefore need trade insurance to cover such risks. To meet this need, Japan must make its insurance qualification terms flexible enough so that trade insurance can facilitate expansion of private-sector capital flow even in cases where the risks are considerably high. The Japanese government should also be expected to help reschedule debts in a manner that produces the same effect as providing loan repayment capital. In addition, the Japanese government should look into providing especially attractive interest rates as a form of assistance when deferring payment to trade-insured creditors. It should also ensure that trade insurance is always available when working out deferred repayment schedules for developing countries.

To be able to respond to this situation, Japan must build up a fiscal base for such trade insurance and, in particular, must find new financial resources for these policies.

(ii) Enhancing capabilities for starting key development projects. Deepening accrued-debt problems have contributed to a dramatic decline in development projects in the developing countries. This trend has also discouraged investment-scouting activities, which aim to drum up and formulate new development projects, resulting in a vicious circle. While respecting the sovereignty of the developing countries, Japan must respond to this situation by enthusiastically cooperating in the initial planning and formulation of key development projects that will best contribute to the host country's economic revitalization. In particular, Japan's private sector can play a major role in cooperating with developing countries to invigorate local private industry, which in turn will foster those local industries that bring in foreign currency. Once the Japanese government has helped stir up the Japanese private sector's enthusiasm toward an expanded role in the launching of overseas development projects, it must actively put this private-sector vitality to work in the promotion of such cooperative activities.

GREATER SERVICE- AND INFORMATION-ORIENTED COOPERATION

As Japan seeks to expand the flow of capital to developing countries with a view toward improving each recipient country's foreign-currency earning power, it is important that this flow of capital be accompanied by a full complement of service and information-oriented cooperation, ranging from consultation regarding economic policy and development project planning to transfers of technologies and expertise for specific industrial levels. Such cooperation is essential from the perspective of cultivating an attractive investment environment which, as mentioned earlier, is a prerequisite for expanding the flow of private-sector capital.

BOOSTING IMPORTS FROM DEVELOPING NATIONS

The first thing advanced nations can do to help debtor nations invigorate their foreign-currency earning abilities is to expand imports of their products. For its part, Japan must continue to make its industrial structure more oriented toward international cooperation and promote increased imports from debtor nations as a direct means of boosting their foreign currency holdings.

WORKING TO REDUCE EXISTING DEBTS

To promote an orientation toward market-based, real-term mitigation of existing loans based on self-initiated agreements between lenders and borrowers (such as Mexico's approach of turning debts into debenture stocks or bonds), Japan has been helping to reduce the existing debts of debtor nations by implementing tax breaks. Examples of this type of policy include making profits earned in buying and selling such debentures tax-exempt, making losses on such sales tax-deductible and working with market mechanisms on a case-by-case basis.

Recently, proposals have been presented which describe how an international debt-allocation organization or existing international bodies (such as the World Bank or IMF) could lighten the existing-debt burden. Although such proposals deserve further consideration in the situation where existing debts exceed the nation's ability to repay, there are many factors that require close attention, such as the problem of 'moral hazards' in the debtor countries, the increased burden on lending banks and governments, and the possibility that such measures may deter the need for new loans in the future. Generally a case-by-case approach would be appropriate.

7. Borderless corporate activities and the new development of industrial policy

(1) Borderless corporate activities

RAPID GROWTH AND QUALITATIVE TRANSFORMATION OF OVERSEAS INVESTMENTS BY JAPANESE COMPANIES

Before 1970
Until the 1960s, Japanese direct investment overseas was very limited. Neither Japanese manufacturers nor trading firms directly invested much money abroad, and of what little investment did take place, the majority was aimed at natural resource development. Projects included petroleum development in Indonesia, especially in northern Sumatra, iron ore in India, the Philippines and Malaysia and copper in the Philippines.

Between 1970 and 1980
Expansion of Japanese direct investment overseas took hold in the 1970s and was no longer limited to natural resource development. Instead, there was a substantial increase in direct investment overseas by Japanese manufacturers and trading firms. In particular, the first half of the 1970s was characterized by growing investments in other Asian countries by textile and electrical machinery manufacturers. This Asian investment boom died down during the latter half of the 1970s, when resource development-related investments were once again on the upswing.

Since 1980
In the 1980s, the invigoration of Japanese direct investment overseas spread to other advanced industrialized nations such as the United States and Western Europe. In the United States, the strongest increases in overseas investment came from Japan's steel, nonsteel alloy, electrical machinery, transport equipment and commercial trading industries. In Europe, investment by Japanese manufacturers and trading firms was active compared with the lackluster levels seen during the 1970s, with the most conspicuous investment expansion occurring among Japanese finance and insurance companies. On the other hand, Japanese overseas investment in natural resource development dried up, with the notable exception of an LNG development project in Indonesia.

Figure 2.9 History of overseas direct investment by Japanese companies

The appreciation of the yen in recent years has supported an overseas expansion boom among Japanese companies. Reported figures for the total value of overseas direct investment in fiscal year 1987 showed an astounding 49.6% leap over the amount for the previous year. (See Figure 2.9; Appendix 21: Trends in Japanese overseas direct investment.)

The primary motivations for this sudden increase have centered on passive or negative considerations. These include the need to secure supplies of resources and raw materials from developing countries, and the need to maintain and expand market share in the face of import barriers erected in the target countries or trade friction and protectionist moves in other advanced industrialized nations.

Recently, however, Japanese companies have had more positive reasons for investing overseas, such as the cost advantages of investing in developing countries, a growing emphasis on avoiding the exchange-rate risks involved when investing in other advanced industrialized countries and the desire to acquire information about foreign technologies and markets to help boost the competitiveness of Japanese products. (See Appendix 22: Changes in the hows and whys of Japanese overseas expansion.)

INTERNATIONAL DEVELOPMENT OF BUSINESS STRATEGIES

In conjunction with the growth in direct overseas investment based on positive motives, investing companies have begun to go beyond the simple tactic of setting up and operating independent manufacturing facilities overseas and are instead building organic networks. These networks link domestic facilities with overseas facilities, enabling an international division of labor based on a division of certain production processes and/or specific product lines. Until recently, for example, products from a given overseas facility were usually marketed in the same country or region, but now more and more products from Japanese-funded production facilities in other Asian countries are either marketed in a nearby third country or are exported to Japan. The relationships between the parent companies in Japan and their overseas facilities are also showing signs of organic linkage as the amount of goods traded in both directions increases. Recently, some Japanese manufacturers have even begun adding R & D labs to their overseas production facilities.

Meanwhile, some of the Japanese companies that have long been actively expanding in overseas markets have established head offices around the world and are pursuing strategies to find the optimum sites for production and marketing. For example, one Japenese automobile manufacturer that has sixty-nine production facilities in thirty-four countries established a new headquarters in 1987 for its thirteen locally incorporated subsidiaries in North America and empowered this new headquarters with decision-making responsibilities for production, sales and R & D throughout North America as well as coordinating the responsibilities for thirteen companies. In 1988, this same automobile manufacturer began exporting cars from overseas facilities to Japan, and it plans to raise its local parts procurement ratio at such facilities to 75 per cent by 1991. In the more distant future, this company plans to make its North American headquarters and its head office in Japan completely independent of each other in their activities. Though the two will be independent, the company plans to develop an organically linked system whereby their activities will be complemented.

Similarly, other Japanese companies are using their own independent decision-making powers to develop integrated organizations that cross international boundaries and carry out activities based on global strategies. As such, these companies are moving toward an advanced stage of multinationalism. (See Appendix 23: Sales destinations for overseas production facilities; Appendix 24: Transactions between parent companies and overseas subsidiaries; Appendix 25: The trend toward multinational companies.)

Although other advanced industrialized nations are substantially lowering their corporate taxes as part of their tax reform efforts, Japan continues to have a very high corporate tax rate, as indicated by its high effective tax rate and actual tax burden. (Effective tax rates are 40.35 per cent in the United States, 35.00 per cent in Britain and 51.55 per cent in Japan.)

Figure 2.10 International comparison of corporate taxes

NEW INDUSTRIAL FRONTIERS TO KEEP JAPANESE INDUSTRY FROM
BEING SPREAD TOO THIN

(a) Promotion of overseas direct investment to serve mid-range goals
As a country seeking to restructure its industry to bring it into greater international accord, Japan looks on direct investment overseas as something that should be enthusiastically promoted over the mid-term future. If the current pace can be sustained for the next few years, Japan will achieve a division of labor in which domestic production will be in balance with exports and overseas production.

As this expansion of direct investment overseas continues, Japan must try to avoid such possible side effects as domestic employment gaps, depressed regional economies and destabilization of subcontracting companies, while managing its domestic demand-led economy appropriately and dynamically.

(b) Building a long-term development base for the Japanese economy
Looking toward the long-term future, Japan must make sure that the ongoing trend toward overseas transfer of management resources does not seriously weaken domestic capacity in terms of production and technology development, something that would damage the development base for Japan's future industry.

Although Japan has a high-quality labor force, it also has relatively high taxes, land prices, commodity prices (with some exceptions) and wage and salary costs, in addition to a complex maze of regulations and restrictions. In the long run, there is an undeniable risk that these negative factors will drive companies out of Japan in increasing numbers. For example, companies whose operations extend into several countries often view the local tax burden as a major factor in deciding where to locate certain activities, and there have been signs that some companies in Japan are expanding or moving overseas specifically due to the heavy corporate tax burden in Japan (see Figure 2.10).

To preserve its long-term economic development base, Japan must work toward revising its tax and industrial regulatory systems, while relaxing certain restrictions to bring its industrial environment on a par with other advanced industrialized nations.

Japan must also strive to keep its industry from being spread too thin by enhancing Japanese R & D in basic technologies, cultivating new types

of businesses in response to the public's diversifying needs and supporting the trend toward an information-intensive society. In this way, Japan
can create new industrial frontiers and thereby build a solid domestic
development base to safeguard the future of its industries.

(2) Corporate management in the internationalization era

RESPONDING TO CHANGES IN THE MANAGEMENT ENVIRONMENT

As the era of internationalization gets fully under way, the following
major changes are taking place in Japanese companies.

(a) Protectionism and NICs
In the face of protectionist trends in the United States and European
markets, and the arrival of the NIC companies, Japanese companies can
no longer rely on the presence of huge markets in the United States and
Europe, or on the absence of competitors with cost superiority, as they
did before. From now on, Japanese companies must develop their
activities within a harsh international environment.

(b) Short-term orientation
Liberalization and internationalization of Japan's financial and capital
markets are changing the configuration of shareholders in Japanese
companies, which may lead to greater shareholder emphasis on short-
term corporate profits. Such a short-term orientation may in turn hinder
long-term, large-scale corporate expenditures or any R & D projects that
involve considerable risks. This may in some cases create strategic
obstacles to the smooth transfer of technology and could also pose major
problems concerning the future progress of independent technology
development.

(c) Flexibility and cost reduction
The distinctively Japanese style of employee-centred management that
has bolstered the outstanding performance of Japanese companies is also
undergoing changes. Traditional Japanese managment places a high
priority on job security for employees, respects employee opinion and
emphasizes employee education, training and teamwork. However, during this era of internationalization, many Japanese companies may be
forced to restructure their management resources by laying off regular
employees and hiring foreign employees to boost flexibility and cut costs.
Such a trend would be likely to alter the underpinnings of traditional
Japanese management, such as strong group orientation and loyalty to
the company that is found among Japanese corporate employees.

(d) Other changes
The increeasing politicization of international economic affairs presents

problems that cannot be solved by any amount of economic efficiency nor by excellence in business performance areas such as quality, cost and delivery. Dealing with these problems will require changes in the way companies develop their business strategies.

To respond to this harsh situation, Japanese corporate managers will have to expand their skills beyond the pursuit of economic efficiency and develop the ability better to understand the social conditions, political situation and security issues of the countries with which they do business. At the same time, the addition of foreign and non-business staff will diversify the composition of the board of directors and top management strata in Japanese companies and will require the establishment of an organization that can flexibly respond to severe changes in the business climate. Another difficult problem will be that of finding and developing the kind of in-house human resources needed for internationalization.

In expanding overseas, Japanese companies will also face an important challenge as they seek to make the most of their employee-centered style of management while striving to accommodate other cultures.

BRINGING CORPORATE ACTIVITIES IN LINE WITH INTERNATIONAL EXPECTATIONS

Japan's rising status within the global economy and the internationalization of its corporate operations have helped bring greater international attention to Japanese corporate activities. In the future, Japanese corporate activities will have a substantial impact on the economies and industries of other countries. It is possible that this may lead not only to trade friction but also raise the risk of damaging Japan's image overseas. With this in mind, Japanese companies should carry out their activities with a view toward preserving international harmony.

In this regard, Japanese companies should be aware of the following four points.

First is the price-formation problem, which applies especially to rapidly advancing high-tech fields. Since an expanding production scale has often enabled sudden cost reductions, product prices remained at about the same level on foreign markets even after the yen's steep rise in value. Overseas, however, such a situation can easily be perceived as 'dumping'. Although this kind of criticism is generally groundless, Japanese companies should nevertheless act prudently in their price-formation activities. They should be aware that the emphasis on market share over cost-based pricing, which is a common business strategy in the Japanese market, may cause friction with local competitors in foreign markets.

The second problem concerns investment activities. For instance, concentrating overseas investments in certain sectors, such as in real estate, might be regarded as very peculiar and unfavorable in other countries and cause unnecessary friction with local societies. When making investments in production facilities, Japanese companies tend to emphasize expanding production capacity to secure market share; however, such practices can create an imbalance in supply and demand on the local market by creating excess production capacity. Furthermore, each Japanese company that invests overseas needs to be aware of how its presence is perceived by the local society, and the company must keep its investment moderate in the sense that it serves no more than the mid- to long-range demand in domestic and overseas markets.

A third issue is the problem of exclusivistic business practices. At present, for example, there are problems concerning illegal collusion among interested companies prior to bidding on public works projects. Such collusion is a frequent practice in Japan. Although this custom has a certain historical background, it must be changed and made more open to avoid foreign criticism. Similar foreign criticism has also been leveled at the practice of buying within corporate groups and at the emphasis on stable long-term business relationships. Japanese companies must respond to these complaints by bringing their business practices more in line with customary practices overseas and must work to avoid activities that invite misunderstanding on the part of foreign observers.

Finally, Japanese companies must do more to blend in with the local society and culture when expanding overseas. For example, Japanese employees working overseas can improve their contact and deepen their mutual understanding with local people by getting involved in volunteer activities. This offers the additional benefits of contributing to the welfare of the local society and helping to raise the image of Japanese companies in the area. Such volunteer activities can thus be seen as vital for the smooth development of overseas business activities.

(3) The development of international industrial policy

DEVELOPMENT OF INDUSTRIAL POLICY BASED ON INTERNATIONAL PERSPECTIVE

The globalization of corporate activity generally presents a strong possibility that policies which work well within the national boundaries of individual countries could lose their effectiveness. This is especially true with regard to money areas such as national tax systems, monetary policies and regulations on capital, where such a trend is already conspicuous. For example, if a country raises its corporate tax to gain more tax revenues, companies may move overseas to avoid the higher taxes, and thus result in an overall decrease in tax revenues. Likewise, raising the official discount rate to tighten the money supply may actually draw concentrations of capital from abroad which can act to ease the money supply.

The same type of phenomenon can occur with the movement of goods rather than money. For instance, if a country encourages downscaling of domestic plant investment in certain product fields to improve its industrial structure, some companies may beef up the production capacity of their overseas facilities and import large amounts of the products in question, thereby canceling out the effect of the drop in domestic plant investment. Another example involves the case of companies which agree to self-imposed export restraints but make such restraints meaningless by channeling the restricted products to sensitive export markets via their overseas subsidiaries.

Thus, industrial policy must now take into account not only the domestic situation but also international demand and market trends, which implies a new form of policy development – an 'international industrial policy'.

Japan ought to refer to the US International Investment Survey Act of 1976 as an example of the kind of system it must establish to gain a firm grasp of the situation with respect to Japanese companies' overseas activities. With a view toward promoting smooth global economic restructuring, Japan should also look into the creation of a program to foster the coordination of industrial policies of various countries.

To continue its domestic restructuring efforts within an increasingly open economy, Japan must be prepared to prevent the types of disturbances that would arise from dumping or other unfair trade practices by foreign firms on the Japanese market. It should do so by taking fair and effective measures, in order to enforce international rules of trade fairness including GATT. At the same time, Japan must also take appropriate measures under relevant international rules to oppose protectionist measures undertaken in foreign countries.

CREATION OF INTERNATIONAL RULES CONCERNING JURISDICTION OVER MULTINATIONAL COMPANIES

If a problem were to arise between a Japanese overseas subsidiary and the subsidiary's host country or a third country, would it simply fall under the jurisdiction of the government of the host (or third) country, or would the Japanese government also be obliged to get involved?

According to relevant laws, each Japanese overseas subsidiary takes on the nationality of its host country and pays corporate taxes to that country. However, other legal documents, such as the Friendship, Commerce and Navigation Treaty between Japan and the United States of America (Article 7), stipulate that local subsidiaries of overseas companies are not necessarily to be treated as domestic companies.

Furthermore, we can cite some actual problems that have occurred in the past when investment-related friction resulted in strained relations between the investing company and the recipient country. There are also local production regulations in free-trade agreements among the EC, the United States and Canada, whereby local manufacturing subsidiaries of Japanese companies are not allowed to operate unless they maintain a certain minimum percentage of local content in their final products. Given these, it is difficult to view subsidiary companies as simply belonging to their host countries in the sense that they are discriminated against because of their Japanese origin.

In addition, while an overseas subsidiary is legally an independent company, in reality it is just one part of an economic organization that revolves around the parent company. Therefore, if the overseas subsidiary is put in a disadvantageous position in its host country or a third country, its parent company will also suffer. Thus, when the Japanese government directs policies toward the activities of parent companies in Japan, it is sometimes necessary for the government to consider at the same time the activities of the overseas subsidiaries.

At present, there are no international rules pertaining to the way in which the host government of a parent company relates to the activities of that company's overseas subsidiaries. In particular, the United States and various European countries have been embroiled in heated arguments over America's attempts to apply assertively its antitrust and export control laws outside its own borders. In fact, a similar problem exists with the US Omnibus Trade Bill's sanction clauses against foreign firms.

These types of conflicts are likely to increase as the trend toward the globalization of companies from various countries continues. Eventually these countries will need to draw up some international rules concerning the jurisdiction of the 'host countries' over the affairs of their multinational companies. For its part, Japan must begin to study actively the creation of such rules.

8. Social openness and respect for individual cultures

(1) The opening of Japanese society in an era of cultural crosscurrents

The rapid progress in industrial societies, bolstered by unflagging technological innovation and the liberal economic system that has existed since the end of the Second World War, has underwritten an enormous expansion of international economic exchange. This invigoration of economic exchange has elevated the world's overall economic welfare, while deepening interdependence among nations.

However, this positive trend has also produced a side current of trade friction, which is gradually becoming more pronounced. Unlike goods, money or information, people and their behavior are not simply oriented toward economic efficiency and thus do not cross national boundaries as readily. Furthermore, it is difficult to change existing systems, customs and patterns of behavior that form the underpinnings of any particular culture. Consequently, we find gaps between economic trends that are oriented toward economic efficiency and political trends that are rooted in a nation's customs and values. Once these gaps exist, an increased level of economic activity may only serve to increase friction.

Therefore, it is unrealistic to expect that the trend toward 'borderless' economic activity will diminish the framework of the nation state. Rather, as compared to borderless economic activity which tends to follow the logic of the strong, the role of the state has, in a way, come to be regarded as highly as ever because it serves as a guardian of the weak. In any event, the global economic system has greatly changed in the past forty years and the meaning of national boundaries has been transformed from definitions centered on, as it were, 'territorial hegemony' to ones centered on the concept of 'cross-permeative economy'. Japan, therefore, has to open further its society to the world taking into account this change in the nature of national boundaries.

(2) Why an open society?

For Japan, a country that depends heavily on the success of the global system of free economies and free trade, developing an open society is a prerequisite for future economic development.

As a result of its ongoing development as a major export market for other countries, as a target for the expansion of foreign-affiliated companies, and as a place for foreign business people to live and work, such countries will become increasingly dependent on Japan for their prosperity. It is hoped that this development will bring Japan more stability and safety in terms of its position in the world.

To achieve new development in the future, Japan must break through its existing philosophical framework by coming into contact with things that are new and different. For example, it ought to pave the way for future success in basic scientific research by attracting the world's greatest scientific minds to Japan and by preparing an environment for the exchange and fusion of different ideas.

Unlike the internationalization efforts so far, this process of 'internal internationalization' will in some cases present a number of difficulties. However, each time Japan has 'opened' itself up to the outside – after the Meiji Restoration and after the Second World War – it has adopted new ways of looking at things and taken on new customs. This has helped bring about prosperity. If Japan decides to repeat this type of experience, there will no doubt be some social disruption; however, if the Japanese continually strive to minimize such problems, the difficulties will be a small price to pay in comparison to the cultural benefits gained.

(3) Promoting personnel exchanges across borders

EXCHANGE OF RESEARCHERS AND EMPLOYMENT OF FOREIGNERS IN
JAPANESE COMPANIES

Quite recently, the internationalization of Japan's economic activities has
been accompanied by a growing number of non-Japanese employed at
Japanese companies and research laboratories. Having foreigners on the
staff not only increases a company's linguistic capabilities but also often
provides an influx of specialized knowledge, technical expertise, and
ideas not ordinarily found among Japanese. Sometimes, foreigners are
hired in the hope that they will provide an invigorating stimulus for the
organization. In any case, the demand for foreign employees is growing
rapidly. But this hiring of foreigners is still largely at the experimental
stage in most companies. To take the internationalization of Japanese
society even further, more foreigners must be employed and staff
exchanges must be conducted with other countries.

Employment opportunities for foreigners in Japan should not be
limited to highly trained engineers but should cover as wide a job
spectrum as possible. Forethought should be given, however, to problems such as the possible adverse impact on foreign relations caused by
recruiting ordinary laborers from abroad, the possible widening of
employment gaps within Japan's domestic industrial restructuring process, the possible preservation of low-productivity industrial sectors that
are counterproductive to an international division of labor, and the
sociological impact of a massive influx of immigrants who seek long-term
residential status. Considering that no national consensus has been
established on these issues, Japan must take a cautious approach to them,
though in principle it has to have an open attitude. (See Appendix 26:
Results of opinion survey on hiring of unskilled laborers.)

INTERNATIONALIZATION OF EDUCATION

The internationalization of education in Japan first requires that Japan's
educational institutions themselves be internationalized. For instance,
although Japan's state-funded universities have since 1982 enabled foreign instructors to become regular full-time faculty members, as of the
time of this writing, there has been only a small increase in the number of
non-Japanese faculty members. Japan's major universities must
obviously work harder to bring in more foreign scholars.

At the high-school and middle-school levels, schools are expected to
continue their internationalization efforts, such as by employing more
native English speakers as English teachers.

Japan also needs to redouble its efforts to host more foreign students
and to strengthen the educational system so that Japan will enjoy a

reputation as a good place to receive a college education. In this regard, since about 80 per cent of the foreign exchange students who come to Japan pay their own expenses and must endure a frugal lifestyle owing to the strong yen and the high cost of living, Japan must expand its scholarship system, provide student lodgings and otherwise offer better support to foreign students. Japan should also provide better follow-up services for these students, such as supplying employment information and helping them keep in contact after returning to their home countries.

CULTIVATING GLOBALLY ORIENTED PEOPLE

When extending economic cooperation to developing countries, such cooperation is far from sufficient if all that is extended is of a material nature. Full cooperation requires various nonmaterial kinds of support on a personal level. Therefore, Japan has an urgent need to cultivate a large corps of people who are able to play an active role in providing such international services. In view of this need Japan must work to expand its responsiveness, while making use of existing institutions such as the Institute for International Studies and Training and the International University.

(4) Internationalizing systems while respecting individual cultures

The internationalization of society goes beyond internationalizing individuals; it must effect similar changes at the levels of systems and customs. Today, as the fallout from various frictions with other countries has come to be felt in Japan itself, it is imperative that those systems and practices which are irrational from an international perspective be fully confronted, and that positive efforts be made to improve them before being prodded into doing so by criticism from abroad. Nevertheless, many of Japan's systems and practices are steeped in its cultural traditions. The major issue in internationlizing Japanese systems will be to find the point where the systems are both appropriate to Western standards and yet also suit Japan's distinctive culture.

It would be acceptable if Japan's internationalization brought a little short-term turmoil in terms of its cultural identity, but Japan should hardly be expected to become completely Westernized. This question of native culture and Westernization is also shared by the Asian NICs and many third world nations. Finally, each nation ought to make its systems more rational and universal and its rule more uniform, while preserving the distinctiveness of its culture, so that together, the nations of the world can build a multifaceted global culture through mutual understanding.

3 Japan's contributions to the world community as a new culturally oriented industrial state

1. Changes in world political and military environments

(1) Changes in international political and military conditions

SIGNS OF A NEW *DÉTENTE*

Following the Cold War period of the immediate postwar years, the Soviets increased their nuclear capabilities during the late 1960s so that by the beginning of the 1970s the United States and the Soviet Union had attained a state of so-called rough parity. A feeling of *détente* flourished during that time, exemplified by the SALT I Treaty and other agreements. However, the Soviet Union exhibited tendencies toward expansionism during the ensuing years, beginning with involvement in the Angolan civil war in 1975 and including the invasion of Afghanistan at the end of 1979. In 1980, President Reagan adopted the stance of 'peace through strength,' and once again relations with the Soviet Union worsened as a new Cold War began to settle in. With relations still stagnant, President Reagan and General Secretary Gorbachev held a summit meeting in Geneva in the autumn of 1985, ending with the longest dry spell in the history of postwar summits. At that point summit conferences entered a new era, becoming virtually annual events.

By the end of 1987, the Intermediate Nuclear Forces (INF) Treaty had been signed, and negotiations were under way for an arms control agreement that would reduce strategic nuclear weapons by 50 per cent. Thus, signs of continued dialogue between the United States and the Soviet Union, which might be termed a 'new *détente*,' have replaced the Cold War pattern.

RAPIDLY IMPROVING US–SOVIET RELATIONS, PARTICULARLY IN THE ARMS CONTROL FIELD

The United States and Soviet Union signed the INF Treaty at the December 1987 summit conference. The significance of this treaty, which was a milestone in the history of arms control, can be summarized as follows:

(i)   it had been eight years since the United States and the Soviet Union signed the SALT II Treaty in 1979;
(ii)   both sides committed themselves not merely to arms control through a freeze or a balance achieved through force expansion, as in the case of SALT I (1972) and SALT II (1979), but rather to actual reduction of current nuclear forces;
(iii)   on-site verification measures were adopted, in contrast to prior Soviet refusals, which had earlier hindered arms control negotiations; and
(iv)   the Soviet Union agreed to asymmetrical reductions.

Agreement on the INF Treaty has given impetus to arms negotiations in other fields, such as strategic nuclear and conventional weapons, and it bodes well for continued US–Soviet dialogue and reduced tension between the superpowers.

In concrete terms, progress has been made in negotiations for a 50 per cent reduction in strategic nuclear weapons and in preliminary talks on a conventional arms agreement spanning Europe. However, optimism may be premature, as problems remain for strategic nuclear arms talks in areas linked to the Strategic Defense Initiative (SDI), limits and verification of ballistic missiles and for conventional arms talks with regard to Eastern Bloc force superiority and asymmetry of armament systems between the two sides.

Nevertheless, regional conflicts in Afghanistan, Cambodia, Nicaragua and elsewhere, which have provided a stage for US–Soviet rivalry, seem to be moving, albeit haltingly, toward resolution. In addition, there is the possibility that greater economic relations may develop between the United States and the Soviet Union in this atmosphere of *détente*. When General Secretary Gorbachev visited the United States in December 1987, he met with US business leaders and called for increased investment in the Soviet Union. He also spoke of domestic economic reforms, including liberalization of Soviet joint-venture and state-enterprise laws. To the United States the Soviet Union represents an enormous unexploited market. For its part, the Soviets need American capital and technology to stimulate economic growth internally. In this sense, the interests of both sides are compatible. (See Appendix 27: Summary of the INF Disarmament Treaty.)

In considering the nature of the international political and military changes wrought by the INF Treaty and other events, we must bear in mind the following points:

(a) Dramatic changes in basic Soviet strategy
The diplomatic and military strategy of the Gorbachev regime, as manifested in its global peace diplomacy and in the INF Treaty, is based on *Novoe Myshlenie* (new ideas). This strategy is characterized by a recognition of 'asymmetrical interdependence' with capitalist countries and by a reliance on non-military means of achieving security. As such, it represents a complete reversal of the strategy adopted by previous Soviet regimes.

However, whether new ideas will be truly implemented in Soviet policy in the face of ingrained political ideas and whether this approach will be maintained over the long term are matters that depend greatly on the success of the *Novoe Myshlenie* movement and power relationships within the Gorbachev regime itself. Such developments will need to be closely watched.

(b) Increasing importance of economic issues in international politics
Underlying the current arms situation is the need for the United States and the Soviet Union to reduce their huge military expenditures (6-7 per cent of American GNP, more than 10 per cent of Soviet GNP) in order to revive their domestic economies. This has become an issue of extreme importance.

The Soviet Union is expanding its economy-oriented diplomatic efforts and stressing its economic ties with the West, while the United States is moving toward true expansion of trade with the Soviet Union.

Thus, the current state of *détente* can be called an economically induced *détente*, brought about by economic necessity. The partial introduction of market economy mechanisms by the Soviet Union and its intention to participate in the world economic system indicate that economies (free market economies) will assume greater importance in international politics from now on.

It should be noted, however, that in evaluating current nuclear arms control, the INF treaty should not be considered as the beginning of the 'elimination' of nuclear arms. The American and Soviet attitudes toward the signing of the INF Treaty and a 50 per cent reduction of strategic nuclear weapons are shaped by their respective concepts of strategic stability and reasonable sufficiency. These notions still appear to adopt the so-called minimal deterrence theory from the US doctrine of mutually assured destruction (MAD). Thus, we should not take recent moves as an indication that the two sides have abandoned nuclear deterrence. (See Appendix 28: Defense outlays among major industrialized nations.)

(c) Economic benefits from arms reductions
The INF Treaty itself will have only a limited impact on US defense expenditures ($289 billion in fiscal 1988) or the budget deficit (Reagan administration expenditures on INF procurement have been about $1 billion per year, only about 0.3 per cent of the entire defense budget). Moreover, even an agreement to reduce strategic nuclear weapons by 50 per cent would yield annual savings of only about $5 billion (expenditures on strategic nuclear weapons have been roughly $10 billion annually in recent years), representing only 1-2 per cent of the total defense budget.

Reports suggest that consideration is being given to reducing US overseas deployment (which accounts for some $150 billion in annual expenditure, some 50 per cent of the defense budget), particularly in Europe. Apart from this, however, because of weapons disposal costs, as well as the increasing need to modernize nuclear weapons and strengthen conventional forces as a result of advances in nuclear disarmament, short-term economic benefits from arms reductions cannot be expected.

PERSPECTIVES ON THE FUTURE INTERNATIONAL SITUATION

(a) A pattern of easing East–West conflict
The pattern of East–West conflict, particularly between the United States and the Soviet Union, has colored all international relations in the postwar era, but we can expect an easing of the conflict for the following reasons.

First, domestic economic restructuring has become the most important issue for both the United States and the Soviet Union, and both sides share common interests in terms of establishing stable American–Soviet and East–West ties through progress in disarmament and closer economic links.

Second, the Soviet Union is now implementing diplomatic and military policies based on new ideas. In concrete terms, we can expect the Soviet Union to base nuclear arms control strategies on reasonable sufficiency and actively to seek closer links with Western economies.

Third, East–West political and economic ties in Europe are strengthening, as shown by East German Chairman of the Council of the State Erich Honecker's September 1987 visit to West Germany (see Figure 3.1).

(b) Increasing US–Soviet control of world events ('Condominium')
Through the INF agreement and negotiations for 50 per cent reductions in strategic nuclear arms, the United States and the Soviet Union, as the

West German 'Eastern diplomacy'
Diplomatic relations established with Albania (October 1987)
Loan made to Hungary (December 1987)
Minister of Foreign Affairs Hans Genscher visits Czechoslovakia (November 1987) and Romania (December 1987)

Soviet and East European 'Western diplomacy'
East German Chairman of the Council of the State Erich Honecker visits West Germany (September 1987) and France (January 1988)
Soviet Minister of Foreign Affairs E. A. Shevardnadze visits West Germany and Spain (January 1988)

Figure 3.1 Growing East–West political and economic ties in Europe

two superpowers, are seeking, in a sense, to reduce the financial burden of their maintaining a balance of power: their common aim is not to abolish totally nuclear capabilities but rather to eliminate their capacities of overkill. Since the Reykjavik summit, the two countries have conducted talks on INF and other nuclear weapons issues without consulting European nations.

In the future, such 'control' of world affairs by the two superpowers will be increasingly seen in the field of nuclear non-proliferation as well as in the areas of space weaponry and production technology, and may also have an impact on the North–South technology transfer process.

(c) World multipolarization and fears of bloc formation
United States. Serious budget problems and currency weakness have led to a relative decline in the position of the United States within the world economy. This may lend further impetus to unilateralism not only in the economic but also in the political and military spheres. In concrete terms, the United States is likely to press Japan and NATO countries to increase defense spending. Moreover, there is a possibility of medium- to long-term reductions in burdensome overseas troop deployments, particularly those in Europe.
Europe. The agreement to eliminate American INF forces, which stood as concrete symbols of the political links between the United States and its European allies, is already having the effect of distancing Europe from the United States, and creating a more unified Europe.

In the defense sphere, there is a notable trend toward reviving the West European Union (WEU) as a means of strengthening European defenses. On the other hand, France and West Germany are contending with England for the role of leader, and there are disagreements over whether to modernize or eliminate tactical nuclear forces. Thus, confusion over post-INF European security issues is likely to continue.

In addition, in the economic sphere, regionalism may intensify as the EC approaches economic integration in 1992.

At present, increased joint-venture enterprises and normalized relations between the EC and Comecon indicate closer East–West economic ties. Diplomatic relations are also becoming more active, particularly between the two Germanys. The interests of West Germany and East European countries coincide, with the former focusing on *Mittel-Europa* (central European states) and the latter displaying greater economic and political independence from the Soviet Union. These and other developments should draw both the East and West closer to form a united Europe.

Asia. Three basic trends can be noted in the Asian political sphere. First, improvements in Sino-Soviet relations have led to improved relations and greater cooperation among other Asian Communist states, including: China *vis-à-vis* North Korea, Vietnam and Afghanistan, and between North Korea and the Soviet Union.

Second, the non-Communist nations are definitely ahead of the Communist nations in the race for economic success. Consequently, the latter are seeking closer economic links with the former, as China adopts an open-door policy toward South Korea, and the Soviets pursue an Asia/ Pacific-oriented diplomatic strategy.

Third, in Asian NICs and ASEAN countries, significant economic progress is becoming apparent. On the other hand, as for the military aspect, over the medium and long term, it can be expected that the US military presence in some of these countries, such as South Korea and the Philippines, will be reduced.

(2) Changes in the political and military environment for Japan

INCREASED CALLS FOR JAPAN TO PLAY A LARGER ROLE AMONG THE NATIONS OF THE FREE WORLD

The growth in the Japanese economy and its prominence in high-technology fields have led to increased calls from Europe and the United States for Japan to assume a level of defense spending appropriate to its economic strength and to make a more active contribution to world security. These demands fall into the following categories.

First, there are demands for Japan to assume a greater share of the burden of its own defense. Japan's defense spending represents about 1 per cent of its GNP, a level below that of other Western nations (see Table 3.1). These demands assert that a nation of Japan's economic strength ought to provide for its own defense and also take an active role in Western security arrangements. In the future, the United States will be forced to reduce defense spending in an attempt to deal with its twin deficits, and in this regard it is to be expected that further demands will be made on Japan to increase its share of the defense burden. Nevertheless, even as the United States calls for Japan to take over a larger share of the burden of free-world defense, it is also showing signs of fearing the increased international power that Japan would gain as a result.

Table 3.1 Survey of Japan's defense-related expenditures* (trillions of Yen)

Category	FY 1986	FY 1987	FY 1988
Defense-related expenditures	3.3435	3.5174	3.7003
Annual growth rate	6.58%	5.2%	5.21%
Ratio against GNP	0.993%	1.004%	1.059%†
Ratio against general account	6.18%	6.5%	6.51%

* See Appendix 29: Extracts from 'Report on Defense Burdens among the US and its allies' by the US Dept. of Defense; Appendix 30: US Congressional Resolutions and statements from major politicians regarding Japan's Defense Capacity
† Estimated from the fiscal 1988 budget and government economic forecasts.

Second, there are calls for Japan to use the political influence gained from its economic strength for the common good. This would involve Japan making greater contributions to economic and political stability in Asia and the Third World through economic cooperation. However, this would also entail Japan supporting and joining in economic sanctions and other non-military actions in certain cases.

Third, there are calls for Japan to use its technology to improve Western defenses. In particular, Japan currently ranks first in many high-technology fields, and since much of its technology has both civilian and military applications it is likely that Japan will face even greater expectations in this area. We have already seen proposals for Japan to supply military technology to the United States and to join in the SDI program. At the same time, we can expect to see even greater emphasis on appropriate control of advanced technology in order to assure that the West remains ahead in hi-tech fields.

JAPAN'S ROLE IN ASIAN SECURITY

As a free-world nation located in the Asia/Pacific region, Japan's position is distinctively different from Western countries.

Soviet military strategy emphasizes the Far East, and the Soviet Union has been increasing its conventional forces there. On the other hand, the United States may reduce its medium/long-term military presence in the Asia/Pacific region, especially in the Philippines and South Korea. Thus, Japan has assumed increasingly greater geographic and strategic significance for Asian security.

Moreover, the dynamism of the Asia/Pacific region, which is absent from other regions, will make it an important arena for international politics in the future. Differences in political systems, levels of economic development, and ethnic backgrounds, along with cultural diversity and complex internal conflicts, may all contribute to instability in the regional political situation. Accordingly, Japan faces growing demands to assume an active role in both political and economic stabilization within the region.

2. Choosing to become a new culturally oriented industrial state

Hitherto, Japan has minimized its military and political burden, choosing instead to work for peace and to contribute internationally through economic progress. However, as seen in the previous section, Japan is confronted with demands to help devise a new security system and to make other concrete contributions to the world community. From now on, Japan will have to choose whether or not becoming a new culturally oriented industrial state is the path to follow. In other words, Japan will need to put greater efforts into defense while maintaining its unique position as a pacifistic economic power. In addition, it must supplement its economic prowess with a new emphasis on culture. Japan must also work to build a new linkage-based security system while developing its economic strength and otherwise contributing to the international community (see Figure 3.2).

(1) Building a linkage security system

The purpose of Japan's security system is to defend Japanese territory and to protect the free and democratic institutions which form the basis for its society. While Japan must possess adequate means to defend itself, it must also seek links with other powers in the fields of defense, the economy and others. Moreover, Japan must improve its status within the international community through greater international contributions and interdependent relationships with other nations, thereby working to forge an integrated linkage-based system.

First of all, within the framework of bilateral defense cooperation under the Japan-US Mutual Security Treaty, Japan must work to develop adequate self-defense capabilities, and it must pursue all necessary cooperation with the United States to assure that the treaty is carried out smoothly.

Japan must also assume a political role compatible with its economic power. In particular, Japan has to contribute to Asian and Third World economic and political stability through economic and technical cooperation. It must also actively cooperate in security-related efforts to control advanced technologies with possible military uses.

Japan must seek to be accepted and even to become indispensable in the international community. In other words, it is not enough for Japan

Old images of Japan	Phase 1. Exporter nation	Phase 2. Trading nation	Phase 3. Economic power (GNP)
New images of Japan	New culturally oriented industrial state		

	Linkage-based security
	Increased defense capabilities
	Greater use of economic, technical and other forms of power
	Establishing international solidarity through international contributions, interdependence and other means
		Developing economic and technological strength as international contributions
		Providing a 'market'
		  Becoming a major importer nation
		Providing 'capital'
		  Three-pronged economic cooperation strategy of assistance, trade and investment
		Providing 'technology'
		  Becoming a center of creative knowledge through promotion of technology disclosure; devising new rules for intellectual property rights
			Forging a new style of industry, daily life and culture (becoming a creative society)
			Nurturing a spirit of voluntarism, altruism and 'enlightened self-interest'
			Promoting dialogue between industry and a society which seeks mental and spiritual fulfilment
			Institutional refoms to encourage creativity
			Expanded scholarship and basic research; development of scientific resources outside major cities

Figure 3.2 Old and new images of Japan

simply to expand interdependent relationships in economic and other fields, but it is necessary for her to become internationally recognized as a respectable and unique nation. To do so, Japan has to contribute both industrially and culturally to the global community, while striving for greater refinement of national character, which represents the mental integrity to which many individuals aspire. From this perspective, it is essential that Japan push for changes in institutions and ways of thinking in order to forge a new style of industry, daily life and culture as a creative society.

(2) Developing economic strength as a culturally oriented industrial state and contributing to the world community

If in the course of making greater concrete efforts in defense, Japan obtains military power commensurate with its economic power (in other words, if Japan were to become a leading military power as well as economic power), it would cause unnecessary misunderstandings and anxiety among both Asian and Western nations. Such a course would isolate Japan internationally and would, therefore, be inappropriate.

Japan needs sufficient military power to dispel criticism from Western countries that it is getting a 'free ride' in defense or that its money is buying its security. At the same time, Japan has to place greater emphasis on determining a future course for preserving its unique position and making international contributions in forms other than bearing part of the collective military burden.

In concrete terms, while basically preserving the free trade system of reliance on market mechanisms, Japan will have to provide public goods by way of economic cooperation, technology transfer and trade promotion. Such measures will realize smooth functioning of the world economy, thereby promoting political stability in the world.

The world has entered a new era of arms reduction symbolized by the INF Treaty and the limitations of achieving peace and security solely through military means have become clear. This also means that the political significance of economy has been increased. Japan's future options, described above, are well-suited to this change of framework of international politics. (See Appendix 31: Comparison of international contributions by major industrialized nations; and Appendix 32: Comparison of value of product imports among major industrialized nations.)

(3) Preparations for becoming a new culturally oriented industrial state

For Japan to gain a unique and positive position in the international community and to gain acceptance as a new culturally oriented industrial

Estimates show that the United States currently has more than 24,000 private philanthropic foundations, which have a total capital of $74 billion (almost Y10 trillion) and provide $5 billion (slightly over Y600 billion) of assistance each year. In contrast, Japan has a far smaller number of such private foundations, and they provide less than 1/100 the level of assistance given by American foundations.

Figure 3.3 Comparison of US and Japanese private philanthropic foundations

state, certain domestic structural reforms must be undertaken (see Chapter 4). Japan must also prepare internally to assume major nation status.

First of all, for Japan to play an international role as a major nation, it is essential that its people cultivate a feeling that the wealthy should share their wealth with the underprivileged, i.e. a sense of voluntarism. If Japan is to be accepted, its people have to abandon the simple pursuit of direct self-interest in favor of enlightened self-interest, which includes a kind of altruism or at least the sense that one's own interests are linked to those of other countries or to the international community at large.

Second, Japan needs to build a multilevel network of cooperative relations in the international community at both the governmental and private levels.

In order for Japan to fulfil an active and constructive role in promoting stability and progress in the international economy and political order, it cannot limit itself to contacts at the government level. Since relations among countries are beset with difficult problems and are prone to conflict and friction, informal dialogue, debate and exchange at the private level have great influence in maintaining and furthering international relations and cooperation. Among Western nations, there has already been active private participation in improving international relations and building national consensus. The same process can be seen in the NICs and developing countries, including ASEAN nations and South Korea. Thus, to foster closer cooperative relations with these countries, Japan must strengthen such cooperative contacts.

Accordingly, it is essential for Japan to provide support and encouragement for a variety of activities, including cultural, educational and human resource exchanges (see Figure 3.3).

3. A three-pronged economic cooperation strategy: assistance, trade, and investment

(1) Defining concepts and strategies for economic cooperation

Japan's economic cooperation activities have supported the efforts of developing countries to achieve economic and social progress. This country feels a sense of moral obligation to help developing countries with the poverty, hunger and other problems they face. It recognizes, moreover, that the international community is interdependent, and that stability and progress in developing nations are essential to peace and progress for the entire world.

Japan has become an economic giant, accounting for more than a tenth of the world economy. As a democracy, it faces the expectations of other democratic nations to use its economic might for the good of the entire world. Expectations are especially high for the promotion of political and economic stability in the Asian region, where Japan is the most advanced of industrial countries. It needs to define its stance in the face of these expectations and decide how to put its concepts of economic cooperation and interdependency into action.

In specific terms, it is important for Japan to use the experience gained from its own remarkable economic advances after the Second World War and make contributions toward the laying of a foundation for economic development of developing nations through industrial assistance.

We shall describe below the most appropriate economic cooperation policies for each world region.

Asia

Heretofore, Japan has placed primary emphasis on this region in its development activities, and geographic, economic and historical factors indicate that this situation is likely to continue. Japan should provide ASEAN countries and China with financial backing (such as the new AID Plan) for their efforts to develop industries capable of earning foreign currency. Japan must also support their attempts to establish a basis for economic and social development. Moreover, assistance must be tailored to each nation's special needs. With the NICs, Japan should make a fundamental shift toward greater private sector assistance. In the particular cases of South Korea and Taiwan, Japan should support a gradual shift toward an economic structure that balances domestic and export demand.

Central and South America

The effects of the worsening accumulated debt problem on international finance and trade require economic cooperation efforts aimed at increasing industrial efficiency and improving foreign exchange earning capacity within this region. Japan should increase the public and private flow of funds by discovering worthwhile business prospects, increasing project design capabilities and expanding trade insurance systems. For cooperation to proceed smoothly, effectively and efficiently, it is best to coordinate these actions with structural reform measures by international groups. Japan must also maintain close relations with the region and support American development activities, which have yielded the best results in the past. Japan should also strive to increase its imports from the area and work in concert with the United States to support industrial development efforts aimed at increasing foreign exchange earning capacity.

Africa

Many African nations fall into the least less developed countries (LLDC) category. These countries are the ones most heavily dependent on overseas aid, and as aid from Western countries has dried up they have increasingly turned their eyes toward Japan. In the interest of international cooperation, Japan should assume its share of the overseas aid burden, particularly in the form of interest-free loans and technical assistance.

The Middle East

Japan will support efforts to establish and maintain political and economic stability in the region in order to stabilize the world's oil supply. (See Appendix 33: Relations between Japan and the Developing Countries.)

(2) Ways to expand economic cooperation

Pursuing a comprehensive three-pronged cooperation strategy: assistance, trade and investment

For industrial development cooperation to proceed efficiently, Japan should implement a comprehensive three-pronged strategy based on aid (financial and technical assistance), investment (primarily direct investment) and trade (primarily imports), all tailored to each nation's needs. In particular, imports from developing nations provide direct support to foreign exchange earnings efforts and thus constitute, along with the provision of capital and technology, one of the most important forms of economic cooperation. Now that Japan's industrial structure is moving toward greater harmony with the international economy, it is important to expand imports from developing countries. The New AID Plan is based on this idea. As that program progresses we can expect further growth of horizontal specialization relationships among Asian nations.

Concrete implementation will require detailed cooperative policies for each country along the lines of the regional cooperative policies described earlier. At the same time, worsening debt problems have led to greater emphasis on macroeconomic and industrial restructuring on the part of international institutions, and Japan is providing more support in this area. Japan needs to improve its capabilities for cooperative economic policy planning by expanding regional studies and policy discussions with developing countries, international groups, governments of other developed countries and economic aid organizations.

EXPANDING THE CAPITAL FLOW

With a worldwide reduction in the flow of capital to developing nations, the world looks upon Japan as the greatest source of capital. For its part, Japan will have to expand official development programs. In addition, to encourage the flow of private capital to developing nations, it is important for Japan to improve its project design capabilities and to expand trade insurance in order to provide risk protection.

EXPANDING OFFICIAL DEVELOPMENT ASSISTANCE (ODA)

(a) Systematically expanding ODA in quantity and quality

(i)   Quantitative expansion. Japan's official development assistance (ODA) ranks second in the world in quantity. However, it represents only 0.29 per cent of Japan's GNP, a figure below the OECD Development Assistance Committee (DAC) average of 0.35 per cent of GNP, giving Japan a ranking of fifteenth among the eighteen nations considered. Japan should assume a greater role as a supplier of international assets and should substantially increase the percentage of GNP it devotes to ODA for levels consistent with international standards. To accomplish such an increase in line with international trends, Japan must work to reach its target.

(ii) Easier credit terms plus adaptability and flexibility. In addition to easing its terms on yen-based loans, Japan should also try to be more adaptable and resilient in the ODA area. Only then can it respond with flexibility to diverse economic development needs in a manner appropriate to each nation's level of development and unique internal and external environment.

(b) Developing comprehensive domestic and foreign aid mechanisms

(i)   Developing and strengthening aid mechanisms. Japan should employ all types of official development assistance mechanisms (grants, loans and technical cooperation) in concert with other forms of economic cooperation, such as direct investment, public and private credit loans and trade. Japan should improve its system for evaluating economic cooperation measures, particularly in regard to the effectiveness of analysis techniques. Furthermore, Japan needs to encourage private economic aid groups and culti-vate human resources in this field on a broader scale.

(ii) Drastically expanding technical aid activities. Technical aid makes up a lower proportion of Japan's ODA than that of other developed countries, and there are calls for Japan to expand technical aid. In particular, training of personnel is vital for developing countries that seek to attain economic independence. To develop this train-ing, Japan should send more specialists abroad, accept more foreign trainees, and provide more overseas training programs. Japan should, moreover, make institutional reforms to increase foreign student enrolment and improve programs to help foreign students adjust to life in Japan. Japan should also improve research assist-ance programs to fit the needs of developing countries and increase the research and development capabilities of these countries.

4. Japan as a center of creativity and the opening of its technology to the world

(1) Japan's current status as the world's manufacturing center

By 1985 the value of Japan's manufactured goods exports had risen to $170.5 billion, accounting for 18 per cent of the $959.2 billion total of OECD exports. In the electronics field, for instance, Japan was the first to commercialize home VCRs, video discs and facsimiles. In a sense, Japan is now the world center of manufacturing, supplying high-quality indus-trial products in quantity to the entire world.

To attain this distinction, Japan introduced technology from Western industrialized countries, revised and improved it and then went on to conduct its own independent development. As a result, Japan now has excellent production and manufacturing technology. (See Appendix 34: Comparison of technology levels in Japan and the United States; Appen-dix 35: Indicators of technological levels among Japan, the United States, France, Britain and West Germany.)

(2) Changes in the technology environment

INCREASED CORPORATE INVOLVEMENT IN BASIC RESEARCH

The first signs of a powerful revolution in technology, which we might even call the Third Industrial Revolution, can now be seen throughout the world (see Figure 3.4). Basic scientific research has become a strategic weapon, and corporations are conducting more of their own basic research. As this trend continues, basic research information is being treated more and more as an economic asset. Accordingly, economic principles are increasingly coming into play in this area.

THE NEED FOR NEW RULES GOVERNING THE DISSEMINATION OF SCIENTIFIC INFORMATION

Science and technology advance and grow through the exchange of information among research scientists. For that growth to continue, scientific and technical information must be disseminated globally in a free manner. However, in recent years, changes in the technological environment have led to international discord. We therefore need new rules to respond to these technological changes, assuring the free dissemination of scientific and technical information.

(3) The choices for Japan: openness and establishing rules

RELEASING TECHNICAL INFORMATION OUTSIDE JAPAN AND TECHNOLOGY TRANSFER

Japanese companies have accumulated a considerable number of world class technologies. Recognizing that science and technology represent the common assets of humankind, Japan should contribute to world economic expansion and progress by actively moving to release technical information (such as patent information) to the world community. Worldwide, the number of scientific and technical papers and talks in the physical sciences, applied sciences, agriculture and medicine have increased steadily in recent years. Accordingly, Japan will have to work to increase information exchange at basic research and academic levels through further improvements in the accessibility of Japanese scientific and technical literature, support for translation activities, and closer exchange relationships with international academic bodies.

JAPAN'S CONTRIBUTION TO RESOLVING INTELLECTUAL PROPERTY PROBLEMS

Basic scientific research information has acquired clearer economic value, and we need to devise a new international intellectual property rights system that accords proper protection to the rights of inventors and discoverers while maintaining the principle of public accessibility of scientific and technical information.

Toward this end, Japan must submit proposals to GATT, World Intellectual Property Organization (WIPO) and other forums to help maintain this new international system, which will expand the role of intellectual

Trends in US Industry
Eleven US-based multinational corporations formed an Intellectual Property Committee in the spring of 1986. The group began actively working with the US and other governments, corporations and the GATT Ministers Council to seek reforms in international protection of intellectual property rights, including patents, copyrights, trademarks and trade secrets.

The EC position on unlawful commodity trade
The EC raised the need for restrictions on the unlawful use of registered trademarks in copies of brand name products as an intellectual property issue. The issue was addressed in the Ministers Council Declaration for the Uruguay Round of GATT.

The position of developing countries on easing restrictions
Developing countries assert that the current intellectual property system based on the Paris Convention is beneficial only to industrialized countries, and they call for an easing of protection for intellectual rights to products. A proposed revision to the Paris Convention was discussed at the G77 Nairobi Conference (1981) concerning restrictions on unlicensed patents in developing countries.

Figure 3.4 Examples of areas of international discord over scientific and technology issues.

Figure 3.5 Japan's standing in science and technology
Source: based on *'86 OECD Science and Technology Index*

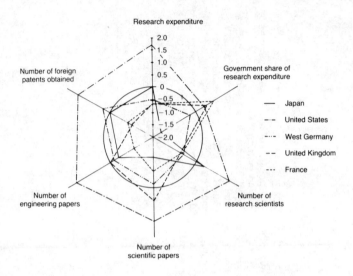

property rights in the world economy. Japan must also endeavour to devise a new set of intellectual property rules together with other countries. Finally, the country should adopt a global perspective in formulating these proposals and, at the same time, be prepared to consider requests from Asian NICs and other developing countries as well as take into account international differences of opinion over the issues.

THE LEAP FROM MANUFACTURING CENTER TO CREATIVE KNOWLEDGE CENTER

Up to now, technological development in Japan has often consisted of adapting products and processes developed abroad or resolving technical problems encountered in trying to reach tangible targets. Thus, Japan has not been sufficiently involved in basic scientific and technical research, and the standard of such research is considerably behind that of Europe and the United States (see Figure 3.5).

In order to expand the frontiers of science and technology and thereby contribute to the world community, Japan must put more effort into the fields of basic science and technology, and make itself an attractive center for basic technical research and development and industrial technology exchange. By so doing Japan will gain recognition as a world center of creative knowledge.

Military	Non-military
Military Military technological development is a comparatively long process. In times of peace, such technology assessment is often limited to abstract performance comparisons, and the market is small. Military technologies are difficult to adapt to civilian needs. 'Spin-offs' frequently occur as a result of human resource mobility, while the technologies themselves often remain secret. Examples are: — B1 bomber, the development of which took fifteen years — SDI, on which ten years has already been spent on research	**Non-military** Non-military technological improvements occur in short cycles because of intense market competition. Cost reduction represents an important motive for development. Examples here are: — Low-output lasers — Laser holography — Optoelectronics — CCD — Gallium arsenide crystals

Figure 3.6 Advantages and disadvantages of military and non-military technology

5. High technology and security

(1) Reasons for the prominence of high technology and security issues

Among the reasons why high technology and security issues have gained prominence are, as we shall see below, the increasing security significance of dual-use technology (DUT), the loss of international competitive power by basic industries important to American defense, and the growing dependence of the US Defense Department on outside military research.

INCREASED SECURITY SIGNIFICANCE OF DUT

In recent years, DUTs, technologies having both military and non-military applications, have come to play a very important role in defense as the underlying pattern of technology propagation has become one of 'spin-on' rather than 'spin-off.'

(a) Changes in the pattern of technology propagation
In contrast to military technology, which since the Second World War has lacked the stimulus of full-scale warfare, non-military technology has experienced rapid advances because of intense market competition. As a result, the previous military-to-civilian 'spin-off' pattern of technology propagation has changed into one of civilian-to-military 'spin-on'. Thus, non-military technologies have recently come to play an important role in arms modernization (see Figure 3.6).

Defense Secretary Caspar Weinberger presents a scenario for long-term conventional warfare to the 1982 NATO Defense Ministers Council.	President Reagan announces plans for SDI in 1983. NATO increases conventional warfare capabilities through follow-on force attack (FOFA).	January 1988 report of the President's Long Term Unified Strategy Committee emphasizes conventional warfare through discriminating deterrence.

Figure 3.7 Signs of emphasis on conventional warfare capability

(b) Changes in the military strategic environment lead to high-technology restrictions

As we move from an era of nuclear arms build-up to one of nuclear management and even the impotence of nuclear arms, modernization of conventional weapons has come to assume greater military strategic significance. As this process continues, high technologies in the fields of electronics and new materials, which are indispensable to conventional weapons modernization, are decidedly taking on enhanced military importance (see Figure 3.7).

(c) Events which highlighted the need for control of DUT

The first Western efforts to control DUT occurred within the context of the Cold War and took the form of the establishment of COCOM in 1949 and the IAEA in 1957. However, these institutions proved unable to deal with changes in the military environment, and they failed to prevent the spread of DUTs as seen in India's atomic bomb test (1974), the Kama River Factory incident (1980) and the Toshiba affair (1987).

Though East–West tensions have eased to a great extent, these incidents sent ripples of apprehension throughout Western countries because they undermined the technical superiority of the West. In the context of the new 'spin-on' pattern of technology propagation, these incidents indicate the need for tighter controls over high technology.

THE CRISIS IN US BASIC DEFENSE INDUSTRIES

The United States has begun to lose its international dominance in basic defense-related industries, such as machine tools, semiconductors, bearings, precision machines (such as optical machines) and computers. The increasing presence of Japanese companies in these basic industries has caused friction between Japan and the United States (see Figure 3.8). Since American military strength relies fundamentally on the domestic industrial base, the relative decline in levels of technology in these important defense industries has negative implications for military strategy and has led to a heightened sense of crisis within the United States. (This paragraph is based on the 1987 Defense Report, see Figure 3.9)

Steel: US import restrictions on foreign-made specialty steels from 1976 to 1980 and from 1983
Special alloys: The dispute between Nippon Steel Corp. and the Special Metals Corp. in 1983
Bearings: The dispute between Minebea Co., Ltd. and the New Hampshire Ball Bearing Corp. in 1984
Semiconductors: The Japan–US Semiconductor Agreement from 1986
Machine tools: Voluntary curbs on machine tool exports to the United States from 1987
Semiconductors: The Fujitsu–Fairchild dispute in 1987*

Figure 3.8 Examples of friction between Japan and the United States over basic industries

In times of both war and peace, the Department of Defense relies mainly on the civilian sector to provide the basis for production of materials needed by US combat forces. Consequently, the Department of Defense must support investment in modernized equipment, facilities and processes in order to strengthen the national defense base.

Figure 3.9 Fiscal 1987 US Defense Report (Excerpt)

GROWING RELIANCE ON OUTSIDE MILITARY RESEARCH

Budget restrictions have forced the United States to minimize defense expenditures, and it has placed greater reliance on outside research organizations (allied nations, universities, private corporations) with substantial scientific and technical expertise. For instance, the United States first sought to perform military research on key SDI technologies in secret within the United States itself. Recently, however, it has called for active participation from its allies. About 3 per cent of the current US defense research and development budget goes to joint projects with NATO allies, but there are plans to increase that figure to 25 per cent by the year 2000. (This paragraph is based on the 1988 Defense Report.)

(2) Fears of rising 'Techno-nationalism' in the United States

The prominence now accorded to these high-technology and security issues and the sense of crisis in the United States over the future of national defense have spawned a trend toward 'techno-nationalism' in the United States.

The United States characteristically wishes to act on its own to improve domestic technology and control its transfer to other countries. The belief has arisen that cooperation among the allies is not enough by itself to stop the flow of technology to the East, and that the United States should exercise direct control over all alliance technology.

Nevertheless, it should be recognized that, even in the United States, a sense of 'techno-globalism' remains strong. By this it is meant that technical cooperation and technology exchange with other Western countries as well as freedom of inquiry are recognized as being indispensable to technological progress. It would be wrong to regard signs of 'techno-nationalism' as the dominant trend in the United States (see Figure 3.10).

(3) Choices for Japan in the field of high technology and security

The various high-technology and security issues, specifically those raised by COCOM restrictions, export restrictions on nuclear materials, the Japan–US semiconductor dispute, Japan–US arms technology exchanges, the SDI participation issue, the FSX dispute, the Japan–US Agreement on Cooperation in Science and Technology and the Omnibus Trade Bill, all demand that Japan establish a clear set of policy coordinates to serve as a basis for policy decisions. Specifically, taking into account the ideas described below, Japan has to formulate appropriate measures to deal with the positive and negative aspects of high technology.

SUPPORT FOR TECHNO-GLOBALISM AND COOPERATION WITH EFFORTS AT US INDUSTRIAL REVITALIZATION

For Japan to foster stable growth and healthy progress in the world economy, it must support elements of techno-globalism in the United States (through educational exchanges, cooperation in technology development, etc.), while at the same time opposing elements of 'techno-nationalism'.

In addition, Japan needs to work for greater technical and industrial cooperation with the United States by making results available from its basic research efforts and by promoting manufacturing investment in the United States.

PRESERVING A BALANCE BETWEEN PROMOTION AND CONTROL OF HIGH-LEVEL DUTs

(a) Appropriate measures to strengthen control over security-related technologies
Japan has become highly competitive in several high-technology areas and in the future will have to recognize potential military applications and carefully consider their impact on security. Acting in concert with the other Western allies, Japan must strictly adhere to COCOM controls on technology transfer for the sake of security.

(b) Eliminating excessive regulations
At the same time, preoccupation with security and an excessive control of technology exchange and trade will undermine the basis of free economic activity, which is indispensable to technological progress. In addition, in order to have effective control, it is better to have intensive

Controls on technology transfer

Materials controls: Export Administration Act
Ban on technology transfer: Ban on technical data disclosure; strengthening MCTL

Access restrictions: Restriction on conference and university attendance, and on database access

Investment restrictions: Disputes between Nippon Steel Corp. and Special Metals Corp. and between Fujitsu, Ltd. and Fairchild Semiconductor Corp.

Increased protection of intellectual property rights
Revised US Copyright Laws: Computer program protection in 1980; extension of patent protection period for pharmaceuticals and food additives in 1984

Act Concerning Integrated Circuit Design in 1984

Trade policy action program in 1985, which provides increased protection for intellectual property rights

Omnibus Trade Bill (revision of Section 337 of the Tariff Act) in 1987, which permits the halt of imports based on the unilateral declaration that intellectual property rights have been violated

Movement to protect trade secrets

Improved technology development
The Young Report in January 1985
This report called for diverse, wide-reaching measures to increase US industrial competitive power and to preserve the industrial base.

President Reagan's State of the Union Message in January 1987
In his address, Ronald Reagan declared that it should be a national goal to keep the United States highly competitive into the twenty-first century. He cited six specific steps needed to improve industrial competitiveness:
    (i) increased investment in human and intellectual capital;
    (ii) the promotion of scientific and technical development;
    (iii) increased protection for intellectual property rights;
    (iv) sweeping revisions in regulations;
    (v) an improvement in the environment for international trade;
    (vi) a reduction in the budget deficit.

The New Young Report in April 1987
This report identified renewed competitiveness as the paramount national issue, stressed the importance of policies to improve competitiveness and called for the efforts and cooperation of all Americans to attain that goal.

President Reagan's Superconductivity Initiative in July 1987
Recognizing the importance of extending America's position of leadership in science into the industrial sector, the president announced an eleven-point policy of support for the superconductivity field, including changes in information disclosure laws to permit government research bodies to refrain from disclosing research results when that disclosure would diminish American competitiveness. In addition, foreigners were barred from attending the conference on industrial applications of superconductivity at which President Reagan announced this policy.

Figure 3.10 Recent US technology policy measures

controls on particularly sensitive technologies even if the number of controls is limited. Accordingly, Japan should work toward international agreements to eliminate excessive regulations and pursue a balanced approach which places equal emphasis on the security impact of technology and on maintaining the basis of free interchange.

THE IMPORTANCE OF THE ECONOMY FOR SECURITY

From a security perspective, increased intervention in free economic activities entails the risk of long-term damage to the security system. In considering the relationship between the economy and security, we must not lose sight of the following points:

(a) The importance of stability mechanisms
We should keep in mind the importance of the mechanisms by which free economic activity leads to industrial and technical progress and then to political stability and greater security.

A nation's security and its contributions to international security cannot be measured in military terms alone. For instance, economic stability is an extremely important element in the security of a nation or a region. Also, economic progress depends on guaranteed free economic and research activities.

US techno-globalism, Soviet *perestroika* and trends in US-Soviet summits all reflect the emerging importance of these mechanisms.

(b) Security through increased economic interdependence
We should note that increased interdependence in economic areas such as trade, capital, technology and information serves to increase security as well.

JAPANESE OPTIONS REGARDING ADVANCED TECHNOLOGY INDUSTRIES

(a) Seeking progress based on non-military demand
Many advanced technologies have dual military and non-military applications, and Japan is confronted with the issue of whether its advanced technology industries can overcome security-related restrictions and achieve healthy progress without relying on defense-related or military demands. Therefore:

(i)   Japan should seek future progress based on non-military demand, recognizing fully that its past progress has occurred precisely in that area, which is one where it can exercise creativity and conduct enterprise freely.

(ii)   Once it reaches maturity, non-military demand will create a vast and diverse market. It can be expected that the proportion of non-military demand, already pre-eminent in the field of electronics, will increase in the aircraft industry, where military demand predominates globally (and accounted for 83 per cent of demand in Japan's aircraft industry in 1986), and in the space industry, where government demand currently dominates (see Tables 3.2, 3.3 and 3.4). (These include, for example, commuter aircraft, air taxis, business aircraft, communications satellites and broadcast satellites.)

(iii)   Japan's status as a pacifistic state under its constitution makes it inappropriate to rely excessively on defense-related demand.

On the other hand, Europe and America are spending huge sums of money on outside organizations, including private companies, for basic military research. It should be noted that there is comparatively far less basic research being done by Japanese companies. The long-term perspective demands greater efforts to spur basic research in the private sector.

(b) Appropriate level of reliance on defense-related demand
Consistent with its status as a pacifistic nation, Japan has implemented regulations in the weapons field through its Three Principles on Arms Export and February 1976 Policy Statement Concerning Arms Export (abbreviated to Three Principles on Arms Export, Etc.). In 1983, however, Japan made an exception to the Three Principles on Arms Export, Etc., thereby opening the door for it to supply arms technology to the United States. Also, in July 1987, Japan and the United States concluded the Agreement Between the Government of Japan and the Government of the United States of America Concerning Japanese Participation in Research in the Strategic Defense Initiative. It is necessary to take appropriate steps for technical exchange and joint research and development with the United States within the framework established by the Japan–US Mutual Security Treaty, which defines the scope of mutual cooperation between Japan and the United States in the defense field.

Moreover, with regard to DUTs, although the pattern of technology propagation is changing, there will be a number of cases in which key technologies move from defense-related fields into non-military ones. An appropriate level of reliance on defense-related demand is necessary for Japan to establish contacts with top Western companies and keep up-to-date with international advanced technology development. In addition, inasmuch as many advanced technologies are DUTs, if Japanese industry accumulates more international experience in sensitive military technology areas, it will also be able to acquire a more internationally balanced awareness and sense of fairness in relation to those technologies. (See Appendix 36: Japan's Three Principles on Arms Export, Etc.)

Table 3.2 Sale of production in the Japanese aircraft space industries
(1986 figures, exchange rate at $1=169 Yen

	Japan	United States
Aircraft		
Total sales	Y622.5 billion	Y9.3600 trillion
Defense sales Percentage	83%	72% (in 1985)
Space		
Total sales	Y171.9 billion	Y3.3901 trillion
Government budget allocation	Y117.3 billion	Y3.2256 trillion

Table 3.3 Current status of Japanese civilian aircraft production

Type	Size	Current status
Airliner	100 seats or more	Development is very difficult technologically, requires enormous capital resources and thus entails great risk. Also, it is difficult for a single compnay to secure a share of the market, so the dominant world trend is toward international joint ventures.
Commuter, air taxi	30-100 seats	Japan revised its Aircraft Industry Promotion Law in 1986 to encourage international joint-venture development. Specific projects include development of the YXX civilian aircraft and the V2500 civilian aircraft engine.
Business aircraft, helicopter		The domestic market is extremely limited. This area is not one in which domestic manufacturers can do well. Market needs will increase with the spread of aviation sports and leisure activities. However, the high cost of obtaining a pilot's license in Japan has stifled growth in this area.
Ultra-light aircraft	Weight of 150 kg or less	The spread of aviation sports has led to the formation of a number of flying clubs in Japan. Nonetheless, there are tight restrictions on the extent of such flying activities.

Table 3.4 Principal Japanese Space Industry Products (1986 sales figures, £100 m.)

Category	Main Products	Sales	%
Rockets	H-1, solid rockets	503	29
Satellites	Communications satellites, broadcast satellites	483	28
Others	Parts for above-listed items	76	4
Earth-based facilities	Satellite communications earth stations	510	30
Software	Data-processing software	147	9
Total		1,719	100

4 Domestic preparations for becoming a new culturally oriented industrial state

1. Creating new styles of industry, daily life and culture

In the context of the previous discussion, Japanese society should pursue the following goals in the future:

— a shift from material to psychological richness;
— a shift from a throw-away to a creative society;
— a shift from a culture which accentuates superficial change to one which puts the emphasis on substantial accomplishments;
— a shift from a 'taking' attitude to one with a higher proportion of 'giving';
— a shift from borrowing from the West to creating new styles of industry, daily life and culture;
— a shift from a 'money game' economy to one which values real investments.

(1) Directions for creating new styles of industry, daily life and culture

Now that Japan has caught up with the West and matured as an economic power, its quest to create a new model for human life is attracting the attention and interest of people everywhere. From now on, new styles (values and forms) of industry, daily life and culture that Japan creates must be ones which will be accepted by and contribute to the human community at large.

To begin with, there has to be a change in the consciousness of the Japanese within the context of the international community. This will involve the transformation of the vacuum cleaner-like absorption of foreign ideas (taking only) into a more self-sacrificing, voluntaristic spirit, in which there is giving as well. Japan must also change its society, which at present values group orientation and self-effacement, into one that values individual initiative and self-expression. Society must change from one with little tolerance for diversity into one with the flexibility to accept coexistence of different races, values and ideas.

At the same time, Japanese society does have some unique qualities including the respect it has for creating things, the running of business and other organizations based on human respect, and the remarkable level of equality which has been achieved in society. All these can form part of a new model for human society, and Japan should strive to maintain and develop these qualities still further.

It will be difficult for Japan to rely on foreign models to create new styles of industry, daily life and culture. A new 'Japanism' or 'national spirit' should be built on Japan's existing cultural essence and view of life, such as its relative idea of values, non-antagonistic concept of the relationship between nature, society and man, Confucian altruism and, in a positive sense, esteem for assiduity.

(2) Building a social culture of longevity

In working toward our new styles of industry, daily life and culture, we must take special note of the social implications of longer individual life spans in the future.

In Japan, the elderly population is expected to reach 20 million by the year 2000. Advances in medical treatment have provided greater opportunities for the elderly to make positive use of their knowledge and experience in economic and social activities. Generally, the elderly are fairly well-off financially, and there is the possibility of a large market forming among these healthy and wealthy elderly people. On the other hand, the rapid ageing of society will require a number of preparatory measures, including increased medical treatment, health maintenance and protective services, as well as a better means for finding employment for the elderly, reformation of workplaces and a fair allocation of social costs among the generations.

If Japan makes the necessary social preparations, there is a good chance it will forge a culture of longevity, which it can offer to the world as part of a 'Japanese Dream'.

(3) Preparing society for new ideas and new choices

Changing values among the younger generation have planted the seeds for new styles of industry, daily life and culture. However, the government needs actively to undertake the following steps to prepare society for a succession of new ideas and choices.

CREATING AN ENVIRONMENT FOR PROPOSING IDEAS

Only within an environment that is conducive to the creation of new ideas, trends and images can individuals or organizations hope continually to generate such concepts.

Toward that end, Japan needs to establish an institution for interdisciplinary scholarship, which could perhaps be called the Institute for Studies of 21st Century Industry and Civilization. Specialists from a variety of disciplines could study together how to create a new society and then propose a wide range of models for industry, daily life and culture. In addition, Japan should promote business ventures in new fields, including such 'cultural' areas as design and fashion, and should further improve and diversify the communications facilities based on new electronic media. Japan must also carry out educational reforms to promote greater creativity.

CREATING AN ENVIRONMENT WITH A WIDER RANGE OF CHOICES

It is also essential to create an environment in which people can adopt promising ideas and carry them out on their own or can modify and improve them to suit their own needs.

To accomplish this, Japan needs actively to promote more flexible work schedules (flexi-time) and job choices, as well as a better atmosphere for intellectual productivity (improved office environment at the corporate level, improved work space at the individual level).

At the same time, Japan should substantially increase its capital investment in social areas to increase the quality of life, such as improving urban infrastructures.

2. Economic programs to correct internal and external imbalances

(1) Breaking out of the money game economy

Japan needs to undertake domestic reforms aimed at making itself into a more creative society as part of the process of resolving global imbalances both internally and externally.

WORLD ECONOMY

In the world economy, a global imbalance exists in the form of polarization between major creditor (Japan, for example) and major debtor nations (the United States and LDCs). The surplus funds of major creditor nations have become concentrated in the money markets of developed countries, giving rise to a money game-type economy. It is important for surplus nations not only to recycle their surplus and funds, but also to make real investments if a fundamental resolution of this imbalance is to be achieved. Surplus nations also have to stimulate their domestic economies to increase imports, and they have to transfer production technology to the deficit nations. In this sense, Japan must change into a real investment-type economy to maintain a balanced role within the world economic system.

DOMESTIC ECONOMY

The same also applies to the domestic economy. Funds have become concentrated in land, stock and other *zaiteku* (money game) investments, while inadequate investment in real assets is eviscerating regional economies. As with international adjustments, Japan has to undertake domestic reform efforts to forge a creative society and to change from a *zaiteku*-dominated economy to one oriented toward real investments.

(2) Mid-term adjustments in the Japanese economy and investments in new fields

THE OBLIGATION OF THE JAPANESE ECONOMY TO REDRESS GLOBAL IMBALANCES

Accumulated debt in the United States and LDCs and accumulated credit assets in Japan and other surplus nations have led to global imbalances. Resolving those imbalances is essential if we are to avoid a crisis and achieve revitalization in the world economic system. Revitalization of industry and economy in the United States is particularly important for world economic restructuring. Global revitalization will require a closer coordination of macroeconomic policies among the advanced countries. However, we cannot expect the American economy, which has made great contributions to economic growth in developing countries by absorbing their imports, to continue to play a central role. Consequently, with the world's second largest economy and the largest overseas asset holdings, Japan may have to assume a new leadership role in balancing the world economy.

REDUCING EXTERNAL IMBALANCES

Japan is expected to contribute to the world economy by reducing its huge trade surplus, a major cause of the world economic imbalance, and by becoming a major importer nation. By opening its enormous domestic market to significantly more imports, Japan can provide developing countries with greater opportunities for economic development.

To do so, Japan needs to provide information and financial assistance, reassess the functional impact of import regulations and implement import expansion programs which will promote economic cooperation to strengthen the export industries of developing countries and other nations.

Direct foreign investment is also important not only to correct economic imbalances but also to improve employment and industry in other countries. Japan will be expected to expand still more in this area. In order to do this, it should work for better risk coverage and an improved information-related environment, and it should ask developing countries to eliminate restrictions on direct investment from abroad. However, Japan must also actively support the transfer of technology to local industries so that local production can contribute to improving the host country's technological base.

Through the above-mentioned measures, a horizontal division of labor between nations will be realized. In the process of this realization, the economic relationships between them should be formed with appropriate balance.

DOMESTIC DEMAND-ORIENTED ECONOMIC POLICIES DURING THE MID-RANGE STRUCTURAL ADJUSTMENT PERIOD

Alleviating external economic imbalances is an inescapable problem for Japan, and the next five years must constitute a start-up period for internal and external structural reforms – a mid-range structural adjustment period. During this time, structural adjustment in Japan should address: how to contribute to the international economy; how to enrich and diversify the lives of the Japanese people; how to achieve balanced growth within Japan; and how to revitalize regional economies. Since the ageing population will inevitably place a greater burden on society, Japan needs concentrated policy efforts now, while the economy is strong and financial resources abound, to meet that later burden.

To accomplish this structural adjustment, Japan will have to achieve higher economic growth largely through encouraging domestic demand. This means adopting active, multifaceted policies in macroeconomic management and other areas, in addition to working to alleviate external imbalances. During the mid-range adjustment period, the correction of international imbalances is expected to reduce a considerable amount of foreign demand each year. Japan will have to counteract the ensuing deflationary effects by increasing domestic demand. In so doing, Japan will realize stable economic growth driven by its potential capacity.

NEW MEANS OF UTILIZING PRIVATE-SECTOR FUNDS

Japan must act quickly to set up mechanisms for directing large amounts of floating private-sector funds into areas which will form the basis for our new creative society, such as new industry promotion and qualitative improvement of living standards. In essence, Japan must reform its financial and tax systems to provide incentives for private funds to flow into domestic demand-related fields.

3. Institutional reforms to promote creativty

Rapid postwar economic growth has raised the Japanese standard of living roughly to that of the West, and it has placed Japan in the forefront of economic progress. From now on, though, Japan cannot depend as much on external models as it has before. Rather, it must explore its own new model of economy and culture. In this regard, Japan will have to push for fundamental reforms in domestic institutions and regulations to change its former 'catch-up' mentality to a creative one.

Most of the current institutions which make up Japanese society were created in the post-Meiji economic environment. In certain respects, these older institutions, mechanisms and ideas tend to stifle creativity and inhibit the effective functioning of market mechanisms.

The foundation of a new creative society is one which will be based on the choice and responsibility of individuals who are continually seeking self-improvement while flexibly adapting themselves to changes in the external environment. To create this kind of society, we must make the following changes in the institutions that have been in existence since the Meiji era.

SUBSTANTIALLY EASING REGULATIONS

The first change that is needed is a substantial easing of regulations. This will help build a society which values individual initiative and in which creativity can be developed to its maximum. Put differently, Japan has to create an open environment in which new ideas can come to fruition and not allow restrictions or cost to impede their development. In addition, Japanese society needs to wean itself from an over-reliance on government initiative, and instead create an environment where individual initiative clearly dominates.

A MULTI-TRACK PATTERN OF RESOURCE ALLOCATION

The second necessary change is to adopt a 'multi-track' mechanism for value assessment and resource allocation instead of the one-dimensional, government-led mechanism upon which Japan has hitherto relied. The current system, in which all resources are first centralized and then reallocated, is suitable for an established organizational set-up, allowing individual priorities to be met. However, it is not suitable for allocating resources in operations that have not yet come into being, or where the realization of a particular project is not certain. It is important for Japan to diversify patterns of resource allocation in order to forge a social structure with greater freedom and individual latitude. For example, more authority should be delegated at the local level and the current resource allocation pattern, whereby all public funds flow through the pipeline from tax collection to the government budget, should be altered. We should also implement measures, including tax incentives, to encourage private-sector and individual voluntarism.

Through this reform process, the role of the national government should shift its focus to devising long-term policies in those areas where market mechanisms do not always suffice (such as the promotion of basic research and management of external economic relations). The government could also develop policies to encourage initiatives in high-risk areas.

4. Improving scholarship and basic research

Building a creative society involves devising techniques for turning an individual's dreams into reality. With its excellent production and industrial technologies, it can be safely said that Japan has made a number of 'creative' contributions to human society by providing low-priced, high-quality cars and other industrial products, such as semiconductors, and by developing new products, such as VCRs and facsimiles.

Although Japan has improved upon production and industrial technologies which have been transferred from the West, Japan's basic research in science and technology is not yet of the same quality.

As Japan seeks to make itself into a creative civilization, it must improve scholarship and basic research both in terms of quantity and quality. It should gradually move from being a world center of manufacturing to a world center of creative knowledge. Japan must sustain its high level of manufacturing technology while placing greater emphasis on research, striving for progress with an appropriate balance between the two.

In the long term, as more companies set up production and development facilities overseas, there may be less industrial activity in Japan itself. In that context, greater involvement in basic research will benefit efforts to lay a foundation for Japan's future economic progress.

(1) Improved research and development as a new form of social capital

Scientific and technical progress is closely linked to economic expansion and a higher quality of life. This benefits both present and future generations. Accordingly, we should treat research and development activities as a new form of social capital.

The government must assume a leading role if technological innovation now under way is to be fully developed. It should aim to increase outlays for science and technology to at least 1 per cent of GNP (currently at 0.59 per cent). The Japanese government should also actively incorporate private-sector research and development resources, where there is eagerness to undertake basic research (see Table 4.1).

Table 4.1 Government outlays for research and development and GNP figures in major nations for 1985

	(A)* Government† research, expenditures (Y billion)	(B) GNP (Y billion)	(A/B) Ratio (%)
Japan	1,867.3	317,205.0	0.59
United States	12,143.2	953,546.9	1.27
United Kingdom	1,080.0	109,566.9	0.99
West Germany	1,571.0	149,634.9	1.05
France	1,510.7	121,301.1	1.25

* The figures in column A represent total expenditures for research in natural, cultural and social sciences, including defense research.
† National and regional public entities are included in 'government'.
Source: 'Trends in Main Indices for Research and Development Activities in Japan', Industrial Technology Institute, March 1988, and 'Comparative Economic and Financial Statistics, Japan and Other Major Countries,' Bank of Japan, June 1987; excange rate calculated at Y238.5=US$1.00.

(2) Improvements in academic and basic research institutions

When we examine the character and overall organization of Japanese science and technology in terms of our goal of becoming a center of creative knowledge, it would be difficult to assert that the proper environment for conducting academic and basic research and deriving creative technology currently exists. In the future, Japan will have to make the following improvements in that environment.

FREEDOM AND COMPETITION IN SCIENTIFIC RESEARCH

In certain respects, the closed environments (the seniority system, life-time employment, etc.) within which Japanese scientists and technicians function inhibit creative thinking and research. For Japan to increase its

| Development of a research support system combining public input regarding research theme and proper evaluation techniques; one such example is the American NSF | Creating research talent mobility by introducing set contract periods for university personnel (researchers) |

Figure 4.1 Policies for promoting freedom and competition in the research environment

creative contributions in the fields of science and technology, it must review existing institutions and consider whether to establish new ones which will permit research talent mobility and more flexible use of research funds. Japan must adopt the principles of freedom and competition in the research environment so that enthusiastic and talented people can freely conduct major research activities irrespective of age or rank (see Figure 4.1).

A NEW PARTNERSHIP BETWEEN INDUSTRIAL, ACADEMIC AND GOVERNMENT RESEARCH

Advanced technology fields will require greater coordination between science and technology than has so far been the case. A system is needed which will facilitate greater mutual feedback between the realms of science and technology and promote a more extensive use of research results. Mutual cooperation and joint projects by researchers from different fields will assume greater importance for research and development efforts.

A number of ways have been suggested to coordinate research activities in these changing times. For example, the government might concentrate on institutional reforms, new facilities and large-scale projects while the academic world could open itself further to the outside and use more private-sector funds. The industrial world, in turn, could work on commercial application projects. However, rather than this fragmented approach, Japan should offer policy support to more fluid cooperation between industry, the academic world and government. It needs to establish joint industry–academic–government research consortia, support databases of research information, and ease regulations concerning corporate funding of adjunct faculty chairs.

5. Reforms to promote regional revitaliztion

(1) Alleviating over-concentration in Tokyo and creating decentralized institutions

Explosive growth in Japan's service economy, information-oriented services and the increasingly international nature of Japanese society have caused the Tokyo area to become an even greater focus of concentrated activity. The area already houses 24.5 per cent of Japan's population and half of the total number of people actively involved in the arts, culture and academia. In addition, approximately half of all corporations with a capital of Y1 billion or more are located in the city. Roughly 50 per cent of all Japan's outstanding bank loans are in Tokyo.

This high degree of concentration results in a disproportionate use of Japan's land area (see Figure 4.2). The following points are worth noting:

(i)   Concentration in the Tokyo area has dramatically reduced the economic vitality in and around Osaka, Nagoya and other urban centers. It has spawned a vicious circle in which talented people leave other prefectures, causing stagnation and further enervation in those areas.

(ii) There are too few railroads, highways, sewers, waste-treatment facilities and other types of infrastructure in Tokyo to support the number of residents and businesses located there. As a result, living conditions, especially housing and commuting, are worsening.

(iii) Until recently, the driving force behind cultural development in Japan has been its distinctive local cultures. Concentration in Tokyo and the accompanying lack of vitality in other prefectures have accelerated the homogenization of the once diverse Japanese culture.

(iv) With so many facilities in a single geographical area, a severe earthquake or other natural disaster there would lead to a shut-down of essential services throughout Japan.

Throughout Japan's history, the efforts of individual regions to increase their own vitality have led to an increase in the vitality of the country as a whole. As one dominant region began to decline, other regions matured and rose to take its place, thus contributing to the nation's overall progress. In the Meiji Restoration, for example, some strong western provinces rose up to establish a new social order as the feudal system based in Edo (modern Tokyo) went into decline.

From this perspective, national development on a long-term basis requires that the current over-concentration in Tokyo be alleviated and decentralization of institutions be examined.

(2) Reforms needed for regional revitalization

The following institutional reforms are needed to alleviate over-concentration in Tokyo and achieve more broadly based national development.

On four occasions, Japan has adopted a comprehensive national development plan to achieve balanced land development throughout the country. The main points of each follow.

The Comprehensive National Development Plan (1962)	*The New Comprehensive National Development Plan (1969)*	*The Third Comprehensive National Development Plan (1977)*	*The Fourth Comprehensive National Development Plan (1987)*
Regional development of large industrial sites through the establishment of new industrial cities and industrial development zones	Development of new industrial cities and ultra-large industrial zones, along with redistribution and dispersion of urban facilities through the construction of high-speed transportation and data networks	More encouragement for dispersion of industry outside Tokyo, Osaka and Nagoya, and balanced development of housing construction to accommodate a large population	Regional development with distinctive features for each region; multipurpose, geographically dispersed land usage through transportation network expansion; improvement of regional balance and interregional cooperation.

These plans have had some effect in promoting regional dispersion of industry, as seen in the decline in the share of manufactured goods shipped from Tokyo. (In fact, the percentage in the value of manufactured goods produced in the Tokyo area decreased from 29.9 per cent in 1969 to 25.9 per cent in 1984.) Currently, tertiary industries such as finance, information and service businesses rather than manufacturing account for the present concentration in the capital city. With the growing post-industrialization of Japanese society, redistributing these tertiary industries will require unprecedented and sweeping reforms.

Figure 4.2 Existing national land development plans

REORGANIZE THE CENTRAL GOVERNMENT AND DELEGATE AUTHORITY TO
MUNICIPALITIES

To alleviate the present situation and develop a basis for long-term
national development, Japan must reassess the mechanism of centralized
government, including budgeting and other resource allocation systems.
Moreover, there must be continued contemplation of further changes to
the system of central government. Japan should also consider introducing a federal system and reorganizing local government bodies accordingly. As part of that process, it is also essential to consider delegating
fundamental and substantial authority to those local bodies.

INDUCE KNOWLEDGE-INTENSIVE INDUSTRIES TO LOCATE OUTSIDE MAJOR
CITIES

Japan's changing industrial structure will give the information-processing service and other software and research industries a central role in
the economy and the best prospects for success. The problem with these
industries at present is that because of integration advantages they are
located in major cities, particularly Tokyo.

LIMIT NEW BUSINESSES IN MAJOR CITIES

Japan has already taken some steps to induce businesses to locate in the
provinces. However, it has been argued that more aggressive measures
are needed. These could include special taxes on land holdings and office
sites, stiffer laws limiting factory construction, and requirements that
companies locating in Tokyo provide housing facilities. However, before
implementing such measures, certain issues such as land use restrictions
and the impact on small businesses have to be considered.

TRANSFER GOVERNMENT FUNCTIONS AWAY FROM TOKYO

There have already been a number of steps taken to move institutions out
of central Tokyo, including the transfer of several national research
institutes to Tsukuba, the transfer of some universities to the Hachioji
area of suburban Tokyo, development of satellite cities, and the establishment of Kansai Academic City near Osaka. Nevertheless, more sweeping
measures will have to be adopted if the problem of over-concentration in
Tokyo is to be remedied. The idea of moving the capital and all governmental functions to another location in order to ease overcrowing in the
Tokyo area merits serious consideration (see Figure 4.3).

If regional decentralization is to be achieved, it is essential first to reorganize the current central government-oriented authority structures and enact far-reaching reforms in local administration. Sweeping measures to delegate authority from some government ministries to local authorities should be considered. Also, as circumstances warrant, certain administrative functions which transcend prefectural boundaries, such as regional planning, should be combined. Regional bodies would serve to unify administration in these sectors, which hitherto have been managed on an uncoordinated basis by individual prefectures.

One suggestion for handling these problems is to abolish the current prefectures and replace them with states, which would encompass several prefectural areas. The new states would incorporate current regional branches of national ministries and bureaux along with all prefectures within the region. Under this plan, regional branches would delegate their authority to the new state government, thus unifying all administrative activities under the state government. The diagram below illustrates how such an arrangement might work:

Current System	National government	Regional bodies	Prefectures	Local governments
			Combined	
Revised System	National government		State governments	Local governments

Arguments for abolishing the prefectures and establishing states are as follows:

● Broad-scale comprehensive development and economic planning are necessary on a regional basis. It is impossible at the national level to assimilate the divergent interests of each region and formulate policies appropriate for each. Yet, at the prefectural level, the governmental unit is too small to undertake sweeping policy initiatives.
● The major cities have almost the same administrative authority as prefectures in terms of local police powers. This creates overlapping administrative areas between prefectures and municipalities and leads to inefficiency. Establishing state governments could eliminate this duplication.
● Allowing state governments to have greater control of administration could foster competition among regions, thus serving to revitalize each region. Aside from the basic framework, social and educational reforms are difficult to carry out uniformly in every detail on a national scale. It is practically impossible to get 120 million Japanese to work in synch when the order comes from above. Delegating authority to state governments would give each state the freedom to carry out distinctive reforms. Ideally, each region would compete with the others in the reform process, thus allowing the most rational and efficient reforms to emerge. In this way, a new national structure would be established.

Figure 4.3 A proposal to establish a federal system

APPENDIX 1: PER CAPITA GDP IN ADVANCED INDUSTRIALIZED NATIONS (US$1,000)

Country	Per capita GDP
Switzerland	26.0
Iceland	21.4
Denmark	19.9
Norway	19.8
Japan	19.4
Sweden	18.8
West Germany	18.4
United States	18.3
Finland	17.7
Luxembourg	16.8
Canada	16.1
France	15.7
Austria	15.6
Netherlands	14.7
Belgium	14.2
Italy	13.1
Australia	12.2
Britain	11.6
New Zealand	10.9
Ireland	8.1

Note: The GDP is based on 1987 figures and population on 1986 figures.
Compiled from OECD Main Economic Indicators.

APPENDIX 2: TRADE FRICTION ISSUES, IMAGES OF JAPAN AND POSSIBLE JAPANES RESPONSES

This material was draw up as part of a committee study aimed at better understanding of trade friction-related images of Japan.

I *Problems that can be solved by government policy measures, etc.*

Trade Friction	Overseas Images of Japan and the Japanese (negative images)	Possible Responses
A. Problems that can be solved by changes in political institutions	1. Workaholics; work week too long	1. Steer the economy toward greater internal demand to restructure industry and correct the external imbalance
1. External imbalance vs. the world, vs. the United States, etc.	2. Lack of originality; applied science is skewed toward copycat technologies	2. Resolve specific cases of trade friction
2. Structure of the Japanese economy; personal savings overencouraged by 'maruyu' system	3. Not receptive to foreigners; very restrictive immigration policy	3. Make a greater international contribution through economic cooperation, etc.
3. Foreign lawyers in Japan; liberalization of international legal practice, full application of reciprocity	4. Lack of skill in communicating with foreigners; poorly educated in foreign languages and linguistics	4. Shorten working hours
4. Standards certification; closing the gap between Japanese and international standards	5. Slogan-oriented; actions do not reflect words, consensus-oriented society slow to change	5. Allot more money toward basic scientific research
	6. Vague foreign policy and vulnerable to foreign pressure; 'wait-and-see' diplomacy	6. Educational reform; improve foreign-language and linguistic education, lay the groundwork for original basic research, promote cooperation among industry, academia and government, liberalize education

I Problems that can be solved by government policy measures, etc.

Trade Friction	Overseas Images of Japan and the Japanese (negative images)	Possible Responses
5. Liberalization of agricultural products; agricultural imports over-regulated	7. Unfair trade practices; no understanding of what balanced trade is	7. Accept more foreigners; affirmative actions for foreign businessmen, teachers, researchers and students
6. The 'Toshiba/Soviet Union Incident'; national security regulations not thorough	8. Inflated food prices; too much government regulation of food	8. Relax government regulations
B. Private-sector behaviour that can be affected by government policy		9. Other
1. Semiconductors; buying within corporate groups deprives foreign semiconductor firms of market access; complaints of Japanese dumping in US and third-country markets		
2. Machine tools; growing dependence of Japanese imports seen as possible threat to US security		
3. Kansai International Airport project; procurement process needs to be clarified and liberalized		

APPENDIX 2: TRADE FRICTION ISSUES, IMAGES OF JAPAN AND POSSIBLE JAPANES RESPONSES *continued*

II Problems that require changes in lifestyle and society

Trade Friction	Overseas Images of Japan and the Japanese (negative images)	Possible Responses
1. Toshiba/Soviet Union Incident*; not conscious enough of national security	1. Workaholics*; lack leisure time	Although such changes will require a long time and will inevitably cause some social disruption, the following responses are suggested from a general standpoint.
2. Structure of the Japanese economy*; stress on savings, buying within corporate groups	2. Lack of originality*; due to monolithic society; need to accept greater diversity	1. Presentation of a vision for the long-term future; the specific orientation problematic, however
3. Kansai International Aiport project*; exclusivist pre-bid consultation system	3. Not receptive to foreigners*; resistant to an influx of other races	2. Broad-ranging relaxation of regulations; particularly in education and centralization
4. Standards certification and security regulations*; different philosophy and legal system concerning the responsibility of the people involved and of Japan as a nation	4. Lack of skill in communicating with foreigners*; they rely on understatement and are not trained as debaters	3. Affirmative action (even reverse discrimination) to hasten internationalization
	5. Parochial attitudes; lack global consciousness and have vague national goals and concepts	
	6. Not very concerned about national defense	
	7. Unfair trade practices*; Japanese industry is overly competitive and collusive	

III Problems that require mutual understanding for solution (problems that require difficult changes)

Trade Friction	Overseas Images of Japan and the Japanese (negative images)	Possible Responses
1. Standards certification* different philosophy and legal system concerning the responsibility of the people involved and of Japan as a nation	1. Apprehensive about becoming a military power	1. Boost overseas public relations information and mutual exchanges
2. Foreign lawyers in Japan, structure of the Japanese economy and Japan's legal system; Japanese social characteristics that spring from geological and cultural factors	2. Consensus-oriented society is slow to change*; slow decision but fast implementation	2. Bring Japan into closer coordination with the United States and Western Europe
	3. Not receptive to foreigners*; they want to preserve their lifestyle and culture and their low-crime, stable society	3. Emphasize sound politics through greater democracy and a market economy; a liberal economy
	4. Have different business customs and social customs; cultural relativity	4. Speak out internationally for cultural relativism; in response to attacks on distinctive Japanese customs

Notes: Asterisks indicate items that are listed more than once. 'Positive' overseas images of Japan and the Japanese would include Japan's socioecomonic system; specifically, management from a long-term perspective, a management style that highly values employees as people, well-managed and stable political and social insitutions, etc.

APPENDIX 3: US TRENDS FOR PERSONAL SAVINGS AND SAVINGS/INVESTMENT BALANCE

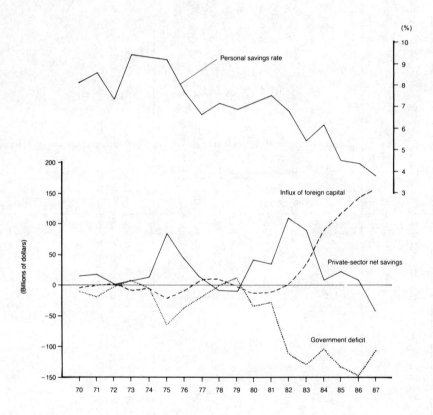

Source: Survey of Current Business

APPENDIX 4: ISSUES IN VARIOUS REGIONS OF THE WORLD AND JAPAN'S RESPONSES

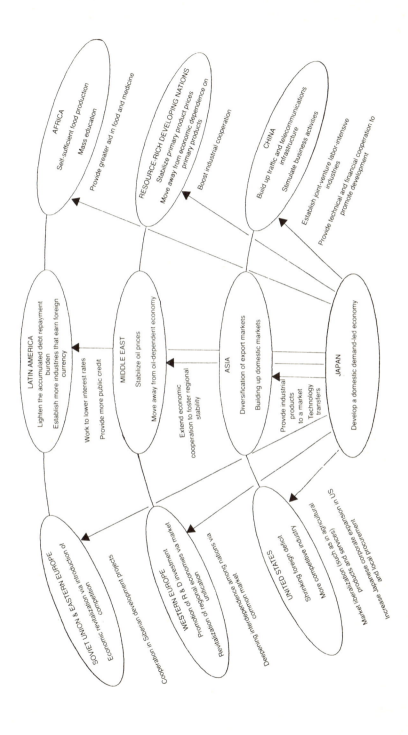

AFRICA
Self-sufficient food production
Mass education

Provide greater aid in food and medicine

RESOURCE-RICH DEVELOPING NATIONS
Stabilize primary product prices
Move away from economic dependence on primary products

Boost industrial cooperation

CHINA
Build up traffic and telecommunications infrastructure
Stimulate business activities

Establish joint-venture labor-intensive industries

Provide technical and financial cooperation to promote development

LATIN AMERICA
Lighten the accumulated debt repayment burden
Establish more industries that earn foreign currency

Work to lower interest rates
Provide more public credit

MIDDLE EAST
Stabilize oil prices

Move away from oil-dependent economy

Extend economic cooperation to foster regional stability

ASIA
Diversification of export markets
Building up domestic markets

Provide industrial products to a market
Technology transfers

JAPAN
Develop a domestic demand-led economy

SOVIET UNION & EASTERN EUROPE
Economic revitalization via introduction of competition

Cooperation in Siberian development projects

WESTERN EUROPE
Promotion of R & D investment
Promotion of regional economies via market unification

Revitalization of regional economies among nations via common market

Deepening interdependence among nations

UNITED STATES
Shrinking foreign deficit
More competitive industry

Market liberalization (such as in agricultural products and services) in US
Increase Japanese corporate expansion and local procurement

APPENDIX 5: JAPAN AS SEEN BY THE WORLD

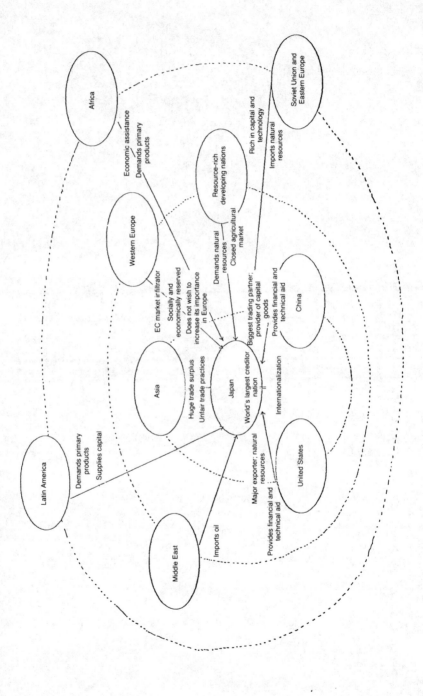

APPENDIX 6: FLOW AND FLUCTUATION OF TRADE AMONG MAJOR NATIONS

Unit: %

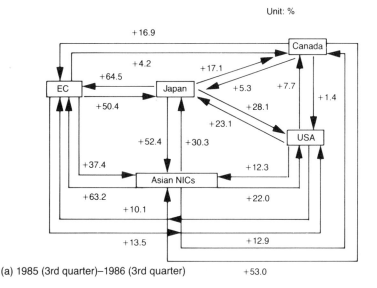

(a) 1985 (3rd quarter)–1986 (3rd quarter)   +53.0

In all other regions, growth in imports from Japan exceeded growth in exports to Japan, and growth in exports to the US exceeded growth in imports from the USA

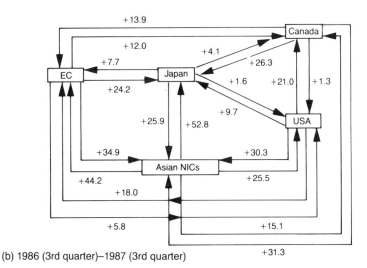

(b) 1986 (3rd quarter)–1987 (3rd quarter)   +31.3

In all other regions, growth in exports to Japan exceeded growth in imports from Japan, and growth in imports from the USA exceeded growth in exports to the USA

Sources: Figures for Japan/USA, Japan/EC, Japan/Canada and Japan/NICs trade are from Japanese customs clearance statistics. Figures for USA/Canada, USA/EC and USA/NICs trade are from USA Commerce Dept. Statistics. Figures for Canada/EC, Canada/NICs, and EC/NICs trade from OECD statistics.

APPENDIX 7: UTILIZATION CAPACITY TRENDS AMONG JAPANESE AND AMERICAN MANUFACTURERS

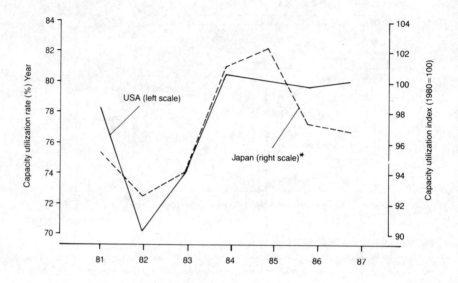

*Japan was a new index based on 1985 figures

Sources: US figures are compiled from the US Federal Reserve Board and Japan figures from MITI statistics.

APPENDIX 8: PLANT INVESTMENT IN THE UNITED STATES

Producers' investment in durable goods

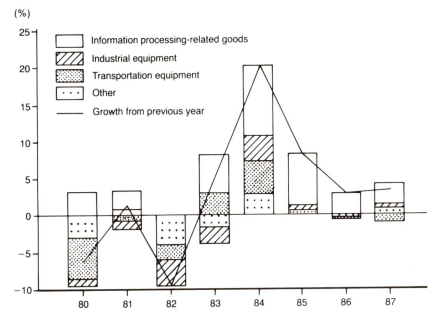

Construction investment (excluding residential construction)

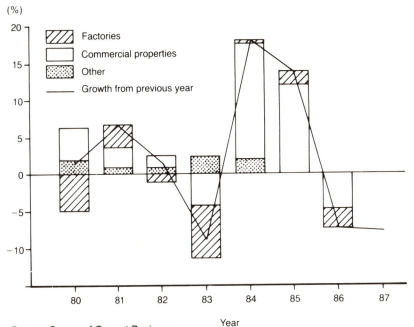

Year

Source: Survey of Current Business

APPENDIX 9: PRODUCT CATEGORIES IN US TRADE BALANCE (US$MILLION)

Product Category	1984	1985	1986	1987
Chemical products	8,639	7,226	6,961	9,344
Raw materials	−31,005	−32,442	−37.695	−39,228
Raw textile materials	−2,150	−2,534	−3,581	−3,994
Steel	−8,690	−8,541	−7,947	−8,039
Machines and transportation equipment	−29,219	−42,985	−70,951	−74,211
Power equipment	1,823	422	331	387
Agricultural machines	221	170	−227	−407
Metal processing machines	−850	−1,510	−1,623	−1,780
General industrial equipment	1,019	−719	−2,986	−3,393
Office machines	3,801	3,366	342	−335
Telecommunications equipment	−11,991	−14,492	−16,749	−16,186
Electrical equipment	−4,435	−5,200	−7,088	−8,453
Automobiles	−24,397	−30.454	−40,301	−42,445
Aircraft	7,903	10,795	10,581	12,392

APPENDIX 10: POPULATION, GNP AND ECONOMIC GROWTH IN THE AISA/PACIFIC REGION

(1) Population and market size

Population
The population of the Asian and ASEAN countries combined is approximately 360 million. Incidentally, that of the United States is 240 million; Japan 120 million; and the world 4,800 million.

Market size
The GDP for the Asian NICs and ASEAN countries combined was one-fifth that of Japan (in 1986) and slightly more than Canada's, but their combined average economic growth rate was much higher.

Country	POP	GDP		PCG	GR	UR
Japan	121	1,955.6		16,162	4.0	2.6
United States	242	4,185.5		17,295	2.4	7.2
Canada	26	363.9		13,996	2.4	10.5
Australia	16	167.3		10,456	3.1	8.3
New Zealand	3	27.2		9,067	3.0	4.0
EC	323	3,461.3		10,716	1.3	11.2
South Korea	42	98.1		2,336	7.6	4.0
Taiwan	19	71.4		3,758	6.0	2.9
Hong Kong	6	37.4		6,233	5.7	NA
Singapore	3	17.3		5,767	6.1	4.1
NICs total	70	224.2	app.	3,200	—	—
Thailand	52	41.2		804	5.3	3.5
Malaysia	16	27.8		1,738	5.1	NA
Indonesia	167	75.2		450	1.1	NA
Philippines	56	30.6		546	0.6	6.1
ASEAN total	294	192.7	app.	700	—	—
NICs & ASEAN	361	399.6	app.	1,100	—	—
China*	1,060	318.9		301	9.7	NA

POP: Population (1986, millions)
GDP: GDP (1986, US$)
PCG: Per capita GDP (1986, US$)
GR: Growth rate (%) (1980-5 average)
UR: Unemployment rate (%)
* China figures for population and GNP are from 1985.
Source: Other population and GDP figures are from Main Economic Indicators, various countries' statistics, and other sources. Growth rate figures are from the 1987 Annual Global Economic Report.

(b) Per Capita GDP (Approximate 1985 figures)

Category	per capita GDP
Asian NICs average	US$3,200
ASEAN average	US$700
Advanced industrialized countries	US$14,000

(2) Economic growth

The Asia/Pacific region's economies are characterized by export-led growth and high growth rate, especially among the Asian NICs.

(a) Average Growth Rates (1980-5)

Category	Growth rate (%)
Asian NICs	6.7%
ASEAN countries	2.7%
Advanced industrialized countries	2.3%

(b) Ratio of Export Value to GDP (%)

Country	1965	1986
Japan	11	11
United States	5	5
Advanced industrialized nations average	12	14
South Korea	9	36
Taiwan	16	56
Hong Kong	71	95
Singapore	123	130
Thailand	18	21
Malaysia	42	50
Indonesia	5	20
Philippines	17	16

Sources: IFS and others.

APPENDIX 11: TRADE STRUCTURE OF THE ASIAN NICS

(1) The following table shows the surge in exports and expansion of trade surpluses in four Asian NICs.

1987 Export trends

Country	Export growth (%)	Customs clearance trade balance (US$bn.)
South Korea	35.7	6.5
Taiwan	34.5	19.0
Hong Kong	36.9	0.1
Singapore	20.9	3.3

(2) Asian NICs are highly dependent on the USA as an export market and on Japan as an import supplier. As a result, all of the Asian NICs have trade surpluses against the USA and trade deficits against Japan.

(a) Asian NICs—US Trade

Country	1987 trade surplus against the USA on customs clearance basis (in US$bn.)	Export dependence on the USA (%, 1986)
South Korea	9.6	40.0
Taiwan	16.0	47.7
Hong Kong	8.7 (Jan–Nov)	39.2
Singapore	1.8 (Jan–Oct)	23.4

(b) Asian NICs—Japan Trade

Country	1987 trade deficits against Japan on customs clearance basis (US$bn.)	Import dependence on Japan (%, 1986)
South Korea	5.2	34.3
Taiwan	4.9	34.2
Hong Kong	6.1 (Jan–Nov)	20.4
Singapore	3.6 (Jan–Oct)	20.0

Note: From NICs statistics; Hong Kong figures are for January to November 1987, and Singapore's are for January to October 1987.

(c) Trends in Asian NICs and Japanese trade surpluses vs. the US

Category	1984 (US$bn.)	1986 (US$bn.)	1987 (US$bn.)
Asian NICs	21.4	30.8	37.7
total	(17.5%)	(19.7%)	(22.0%)
Japan	36.9	58.6	59.8
	(30.1%)	(37.5%)	(34.9%)

Note: Percentages in parentheses show share of US trade deficit.
Source: Taken from US customs clearance statistics.

(3) Characteristucs of Asian NIC trade with Japan

The strong yen has led to a rapid expansion of Japanese imports of Asian NIC products centered on manufactured goods. In 1987, Asian NIC imports in Japan jumped to 50 per cent.

Regardless of the strong yen, Japanese expansion among Asian NICs continued to grow. This is partly because the steady growth of Asian NIC exports required expansion of their imports of capital goods and intermediate goods from Japan.

As a result, Japan's trade surplus with the Asian NICs expanded (except with South Korea). However, Japan's imports of Asian NIC products grew at a faster rate than its exports to Asian NICs, and thus there appears to be a desirable trend toward correcting the trade gap.

(a) Percentage growth rate of Japanese exports and imports vs. Asian NICs

Country	Growth rate of Japanese exports	Growth rate of Japanese imports
South Korea	26.2	52.7
Taiwan	44.5	51.9
Hong Kong	24.1	45.4
Singapore	31.3	40.7

Source: Taken from customs clearance statistics in 1987.

(b) Value of Japan's Export Surpluses vs. Asian NICs (US$bn.)

Country	1985	1986	1987
South Korea	3.0	5.2	5.1
Taiwan	1.6	3.2	4.2
Hong Kong	5.7	6.1	7.3
Singapore	2.3	3.1	3.9

Source: Taken from Japanese customs clearance statistics.

APPENDIX 12: EVALUATION OF OPTIONS FOR CHANGING THE WORLD CURRENCY SYSTEM

(1) Positive target zone

Although the adoption of a positive target zone would be advantageous for stabilizing exchange rates, the following problems concerning its feasibility make it difficult to adopt it during this time of large imbalances among various nations.

The first problem is that it would be very difficult to find a clear target zone that all participating nations could agree on, since the imbalances between nations are so large and the relative advantages and disadvantages of any proposed target zone so complicated. Even if some provisional target zone were established, it would be difficult to build a basic framework for determining each participating nation's responsibility for maintaining the established zone.

The second problem concerns the fact that in today's world, where huge sums of capital are transferred internationally, it would be quite difficult to maintain a certain exchange-rate level by such means as coordinated intervention and coordinated government policies. It is quite likely that setting and adjusting target zones will not suffice to keep abreast of market trends, and any such gap would give rise to speculative capital transfers based on adjustment expectations which could actually work to destabilize exchange markets even more.

(2) Multiple key currency system (tripolar currency system)

Now that the US dollar, the erstwhile key currency, has become drastically weakened, other major currencies such as the yen and the West German mark should begin playing a more important role within a multiple key currency system. However, the establishment of such a system presents the following problems. (The currency exchange market among the several key currencies would have to be based on an exchange level established in relation to purchasing power parity and would have to be uniformly manageable by mutual government monetary policies.)

First, the management of monetary policies to maintain stability among the key currencies (the US dollar, Japanese yen, and West German mark) must deal with quite different political and economic conditions in each of the key-currency countries, which is quite unlike the European Community, for example, where there is a high degree of economic interdependence (horizontal division of labor) and an orientation toward a common market. Since the United States, Japan, and the EC tend to oppose one another on their many relative advantages and disadvantges, it would be questionable whether their three currencies could actually be uniformly managed under coordinated government monetary policies.

The second problem is that, contrary to the view that having several key currencies would divide up exchange-rate expectations among traders, and thus would help stabilize the market, it could well be that this would lead to evaluation of certain key currencies as 'good' currencies and others as 'bad,' whereupon currency traders would speculate based on such evaluations, possibly resulting in even greater exchange-rate instability than we already have.

(3) Fixed-rate system (gold standard or adjustable peg)

Under today's conditions of extremely volatile international capital trends, it would be very difficult to restore the exchange rate system to a fixed-rate system based on the gold standard or an adjustable peg. If we look at the speculative capital transfers that precipitated the demise of the Bretton Woods system (an adjustable peg system), we can see that today's speculative trends are markedly worse. Therefore, it is highly unlikely that returning to a fixed-rate system is possible.

(4) Regional currencies or a global currency

The globalization of corporate activities and progress in international coordination of government policy has produced a much higher degree of interdependence or borderlessness among nations. Given this situation, one long-term proposal that is worth considering is to depart from our current orientation toward using major national currencies as international currencies, and instead develop from scratch an international currency (such as a regional currency or global currency) that would provide an international measure of value, a means of sanction and a way to preserve currency value. In this sense, we might wonder how the IMF's system of Special Drawing Rights, which is now applied to supplement the reserve assets of the ECU (European Currency Unit), a budding regional currency, as well as those of gold and US dollars, might be applied to such global currency.

APPENDIX 13: CURRENCY-SPECIFIC DISTRIBUTION RATIOS OF MONETARY AUTHORITIES' FOREIGN CURRENCY HOLDINGS: PERCENTAGES

Year	1979	1980	1981	1982	1983	1984	1985	1986
US Dollar	73.2	67.3	71.6	70.7	71.5	69.5	64.5	66.6
German Mark	12.5	15.2	13.2	12.7	11.9	12.6	15.3	14.8
Japanese Yen	3.6	4.4	4.2	4.7	4.9	5.7	7.5	6.9
British Pound	2.0	3.0	2.2	2.5	2.7	3.0	3.1	2.4
Swiss Franc	2.5	3.2	2.8	2.8	2.4	2.1	2.3	1.6
French Franc	1.3	1.7	1.4	1.3	1.1	1.1	1.3	1.3
Others	4.8	5.2	4.6	5.3	5.4	6.1	5.9	6.5

Note: The figures are based on all IMF member nations.
Source: IMF Annual Report.

APPENDIX 14: EVALUATION OF RESPONSE MEASURES AND PROPOSALS

(1) IMF-oriented debt repayment system

In effect since the debt crisis of 1982, this is a system that deals with short-term liquidity problems centered on debt problems, in which a debtor nation makes an agreement with the IMF to devise for itself an economic adjustment package, or IMF conditionality, whose implementation is required as a precondition for IMF 'standby' financing. This IMF financing is called 'standby' because it is not extended, but is instead reserved as a guarantee that private banks can regard 'collateral' to support the rescheduling of outstanding loan liabilities and the provision of new financing.

This system's implementation allowed the world to escape the debt crisis and produced some balance of payments improvement among deeply indebted nations, but their austerity policies resulted in reduced imports and a drying up of investment capital. Furthermore, these preconditional economic adjustment packages were short on mid-range measures such as industrial policies and restructuring policies, and this drawback inevitably led to lower per-capita income averages in debtor nations, particularly those in Latin America. Eventually, the people of those nations grew unhappy with the system and some, such as Peru and Brazil, are now politically opposed to it.

(2) The Baker proposals

Given the impasse reached by this IMF-oriented debt repayment system, in October 1985 the then US Treasury Secretary James Baker presented the IMF and World Bank with a growth-oriented 'Program for Sustained Growth' which made improvement of debtor nations' ability to repay their debts in the mid-range future the basis for resolving the problem of debt accumulation. This plan was targeted at the world's fifteen most indebted nations and contained three main pillars: comprehensive macroeconomic and restructuring policies to be adopted by the debtor nations, expanded financing (US$3 billion more per year) from international financial institutions (the World Bank and the Inter-American Development Bank), and additional new loans (US$20 billion per year in total) from private banks.

Later, the growth-oriented approach of Baker's proposals was reflected in the March 1986 founding of the IMF's restructuring facility and the September 1986 implementation of a debt redress package that included growth-oriented economic rehabilitation plans. However, the new private loans that were called for as one of the Baker's proposals' three pillars never materialized in the amounts expected. In 1986, the private lenders had an excess allowance for doubtful accounts and, in 1987, several large US banks including Citicorp, the largest American bank, began amassing bad-debt allowances. Since then, the situation has made it increasingly difficult for private banks to take the initiative in providing new loans.

(3) The menu approach

In September 1987, US Treasury Secretary Baker again went before an IMF/World Bank council to propose a 'menu approach' consisting of a series of finance schemes. This menu approach has been principally aimed at offerng incentives to encourage private banks to provide new credit, and as such it was meant to complement rather than replace the original Baker Proposals.

Actually, the menu approach has not resulted in anything other than the conversion of debts into stocks. Such debt conversion has been limited to suitable investment projects and has been severely restricted by inflation, currency devaluation, and other problems related to investment environments in developing countries. Nevertheless, debt conversion into stock offers some advantages for creditor banks, debtor nations, investors, and intermediary banks, and, as of June 1987, such conversion has yielded US$6 billion and is expected to have correspondingly positive effects.

The so-called 'Mexico approach' of debt conversion into credit was implemented in February 1988 as a system by which debts can actually be mitigated in line with market mechanisms. The future of this type of menu approach will be watched closely.

(4) Mitigation of existing debts by government policy measures

Given the current situation in which mammoth accumulated debts centered on the most heavily indebted nations has reached a level where the burden for repayment of principal and interest now exceeds the debtor nations' ability to pay, there is growing acknowledgement that any new loans would be pointless, and that instead it is important to find some means of reducing the existing debt burden. In addition to the systems such as the 'Mexico System' that take advantage of market mechanisms to reduce debts in real terms, the following kinds of government policy-based debt mitigation proposals have also been put forward. However, such proposals place a heavy burden on bank management and on the debtor nation's fiscal administration, and are very likely to close the door on any possibility of new loans in the future. Furthermore, these proposals involve moral hazards for the debtor nations, and therefore require extreme caution when being implemented.

The Bradley proposal

Presented by US Senator Bill Bradley at the 1986 Economic Ministers' Summit, this proposal provides a 3 per cent discount on interest payments and a 3 per cent reduction of principal over three years on the condition that each participating debtor nation implements economic reforms. The Bradley proposal is also characterized by its linkage of the debt problem with trade in view of the fact that the accumulated debt issue is one of the causes of America's worsening trade deficit and by its call for measures to deal with this relationship.

The Sachs proposal

This proposal revises the uniformity of the Bradley Proposal by adopting more objective basic indices, such as declines in per-capita GDP, and by being more selective and limited in forgiving portions of outstanding debts owed by debtor nations. It also offers lenders preferential repayment rights as an incentive for extending new loans.

International debt allocation organization plan

There have been many variations of this plan, but the basic scheme calls for the advanced industrialized nations to sponsor the establishment of an international organization (or else by using the World Bank or IMF) in such a way that this organization will allow banks to exchange their loan claims against heavily indebted nations for bonds issued by this same organization. (The exchange rate for this would be based on the circulating prices of the loan claims.) Then the organization would allow the debtor nations in question to have their loan principle and interest mitigated or rescheduled on the condition that such measures would improve their ability to repay their debts. In addition, the plan would allow participating banks to receive tax-free amortization of their exchange losses, and also offers other measures such as granting preferential repayment rights to banks that extend new loans.

(5) Capital recycling measures

In December 1986, Japan, as the world's largest creditor nation, put forth US$10 billion in capital recycling measures centered on investments and loans. This was followed in May 1987 by a further contribution of US$20 billion in emergency economic measures consisting of untied loans with the export-import bank in Japan, cooperative financing with the World

Bank, bilateral loans from the Overseas Economic Cooperation Fund, and capital to establish a special Japanese fund for use by the World Bank and other institutions. As of the end of March 1988, about 60 per cent of these funds has been given concrete application. Although these measures have sparked high hopes among the developing nations, most of the US$20 billion used in capital recycling measures is earmarked as loan funds to be provided via the import-export bank of Japan and other institutions, and many countries are looking to those institutions for more liberal financing.

APPENDIX 15: PRINCIPAL DEBT INDICATORS AMONG MAJOR DEBTOR NATIONS: PERCENTAGES

	1980	1981	1982	1983	1984	1985	1986
Ratio of outstanding debts to GNP	33.5	37.1	46.3	57.9	58.6	60.3	60.8
Ratio of outstanding debts to exports of goods and services	176.4	209.2	268.4	304.9	284.7	303.3	356.5
Ratio of foreign currency reserves to imports of goods and services	4.3	3.0	2.4	3.0	3.7	4.0	3.7
Debt service ratio (DSR)	18.1	20.0	24.9	24.7	23.1	26.1	29.0
Interest payment ratio (IPR)	8.8	10.3	14.3	15.0	15.0	17.1	18.7

DSR: ratio of the value of exports to payments of principal and interest.
IPR: ratio of the value of exports to payments of interest only.
Source: 'World Debt Table (1987-88),' World Bank.

APPENDIX 16: ACCUMULATED DEBTS AMONG DEVELOPING COUNTRIES (US$BN.)

	1980	1981	1982	1983	1984	1985	1986	1987
Outstanding debts among nations reported to the World Bank	579.4	672.0	745.2	807.8	876.8	949.1	1,021.2	1,085.0
(1) Major loan categories								
Official liabilities and officially guaranteed liabilities	359.1	402.6	454.7	528.0	603.2	682.4	780.4	—
Private-sector liabilities without official guarantees	74.5	95.5	102.2	111.3	110.6	101.2	90.3	—
(2) Groups of debtor nations								
Heavily indebted nations (17 nations)	287.6	349.6	389.7	421.0	437.6	452.1	471.7	485.0
Impoverished sub-Saharan African nations (28 nations)	32.7	36.3	38.5	41.6	43.0	49.5	55.3	—
(3) Loan sources								
[1] Long-term debts								
Official funding sources	162.0	181.0	200.0	222.0	257.0	296.0	343.0	375.0
Private funding sources	268.0	317.0	357.0	417.0	457.0	489.0	528.0	555.0
[2] Heavily indebted nations								
Official funding sources	37.2	42.7	47.9	57.0	62.6	73.5	91.6	124.6
Private funding sources	109.6	126.8	151.2	193.0	217.0	234.5	262.8	360.4
[3] Impoverished sub-Saharan African nations								
Official funding sources	19.1	21.5	23.9	27.7	29.3	34.1	39.9	—
Private funding sources	6.9	7.4	7.2	6.1	5.7	5.8	5.9	—

Note: Sections (1) and (3) [1] include long-term debts only; sections (3) [2] and [3] contain only official debts and officially guaranteed debts within long-term debts. The 1987 figure for section (3) [2] is an estimate based on all debts.
Source: 'World Debt Table (1987-88)', World Bank

APPENDIX 17: JAPAN'S ECONOMIC COOPERATION RECORD (BASED ON NET EXPENDITURES, US$MILLION)

	1975	1980	1983	1984	1985	1986
Official development assistance						
Bilateral donations	202	653	993	1,064	1,185	1,703
Gratis capital cooperation	115	375	535	543	636	855
Technical cooperation, etc.	87	278	458	521	549	849
Loans, etc.	649	1,308	1,432	1,363	1,372	2,143
Total	850	1,961	2,425	2,427	2,557	3,846
Disbursements and contributions to international organizations	297	1,343	1,363	1,891	1,240	1,788
Total	1,148	3,301	3,761	4,319	3,797	5,634
[Ratio to GNP (%)]	[0.23]	[0.32]	[0.32]	[0.34]	[0.29]	[0.29]
Other official funds						
Export credit (beyond one year)	339	823	472	493	152	858
Direct investment financing, etc.	1,016	767	1,442	380	1	332
Financing to international institutions	15	112	41	130	148	198
Total	1,370	1,478	1,954	743	302	724
Private funds						
Export credit (beyond one year)	83	74	2,069	665	994	273
Direct investments	233	906	433	1,489	1,046	2,902
Other, such as bilateral securities investments	40	660	4,840	6,828	6,705	5,315
Financing to international institutions	7	318	1,574	2,306	2,575	1,326
Total	363	1,958	4,779	9,968	9,332	9,817
Donations from nonprofit group	10	26	30	41	101	82
Grand total	2,890	6,766	10,523	15,070	12,928	14,809
[Ratio to GNP (%)]	[0.58]	[0.65]	[0.91]	[1.20]	[0.97]	[0.75]
cf. Total export credits	422	897	1,597	162	1,166	585
cf. Total direct investments, etc.	1,249	1,673	1,874	1,869	1,044	3,234

Source: 'Development Cooperation,' DAC [Development Assistance Committee]

APPENDIX 18: COMPARISON OF ODA RESULTS AMONG DAC NATIONS, 1986

Ranking in ODA ratio to GNP	Country	Total ODA (US$m)	Ratio to GNP	Overall grant element
1	Norway	798	1.20	99.4
2	Netherlands	1,740	1.01	97.6
3	Denmark	695	0.89	97.4
4	Sweden	1,090	0.85	99.5
5	France*	5,105	0.72	89.1
6	Belgium	549	0.49	97.6
7	Canada	1,695	0.48	99.9
8	Australia	752	0.47	100.0
9	Finland	313	0.45	98.4
10	West Germany	3,832	0.43	88.9
11	Italy	2,404	0.40	96.0
12	Britain	1,750	0.32	100.0
13	Switzerland	422	0.30	99.2
14	New Zealand	75	0.30	100.0
15	Japan	5,634	0.29	81.7
16	Ireland	62	0.28	100.0
17	United States	9,564	0.23	96.8
18	Austria	198	0.21	91.8
	DAC Total	36,678	0.35	93.2

*This amount includes France's assistance to French overseas dominions and overseas prefectures. If these areas were excluded, France's ODA would total US$3,508 million, which corresponds to 0.49% of its GNP.
Source: 'Development Cooperation,' DAC.

APPENDIX 19: COMPARISON OF ODA AVERAGES FOR JAPAN AND DAC NATIONS OVERALL

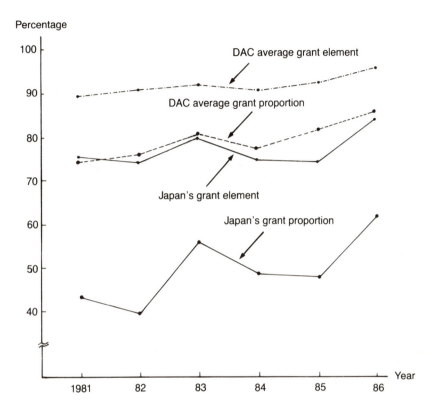

Source: 'Development Cooperation,' DAC.

APPENDIX 20: THE STRUCTURE OF TRADE INSURANCE

Since the ordinary export insurance system was first established in 1950 as a system based on the Export Insurance Law (currently the International Trade Insurance Law), the system has been successively expanded to where it now includes the following eight types of export insurance. In addition, other types of insurance, such as 'technical assistance insurance' which combines export proceeds insurance with overseas investment insurance, have also been established.

(1) Export proceeds insurance: covers losses resulting from inability to collect proceeds after exports (such as plant equipment exports) have been shipped.

(2) Ordinary export insurance: mainly covers losses resulting from inability to export prior to shipping.

(3) Export bill insurance: covers losses incurred by banks, resulting from unpaid documentary bills after shipping.

(4) Export guarantee insurance: covers losses incurred by banks resulting from wrongfully confiscated bonds related to exports (such as plant equipment exports).

(5) Exchange-rate fluctuation insurance: covers losses of exporters for exports (such as plant equipment) affected by exchange-rate differences.

(6) Prepaid import insurance: covers losses resulting from inability to collect prepaid import cargo proceeds.

(7) Intermediary trade insurance: covers losses resulting from inability to collect proceeds after shipping intermediate exports.

(8) Overseas investment insurance: covers losses resulting from expropriation, war, remittance risks, and bankruptcy related to an overseas company receiving investment funds.

Note: Share of insurance types in overall coverage.

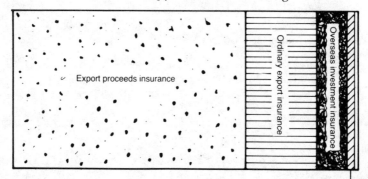

Export bill insurance
2.0%

APPENDIX 21: TRENDS IN JAPANESE OVERSEAS DIRECT INVESTMENT (US$M)

	1981	1982	1983	1984	1985	1986
Manufacturing industries	2,305	2,076	2,588	2,505	2,352	3,806
Commerce	1,174	1,899	1,164	1,482	1,550	1,861
Finance and insurance	843	533	1,167	2,085	3,805	7,240
Real Estate	167	354	375	430	1,207	3,997
Others	4,442	2,841	2,851	3,653	3,304	5,416
Total	8,932	7,703	8,145	10,155	12,217	22,320

Breakdown of Manufacturing Industries

	1981	1982	1983	1984	1985	1986
Total	2,305	2,076	2,588	2,505	2,352	3,806
Foods	142	78	77	118	90	127
Textiles	92	67	174	85	28	63
Lumber & paper	65	76	91	115	15	57
Chemicals	228	322	450	223	133	355
Steel & nonsteel alloys	521	468	479	718	385	328
General machinery	207	164	169	185	352	626
Electrical equipment	475	267	502	409	513	987
Transportation equipment	406	439	486	437	627	828
Others	169	195	160	215	208	435

Source: Japanese Ministry of Finance.

APPENDIX 22: CHANGES IN THE HOWS AND WHYS OF JAPANESE OVERSEAS EXPANSION

Why Japanese companies have established overseas production facilities

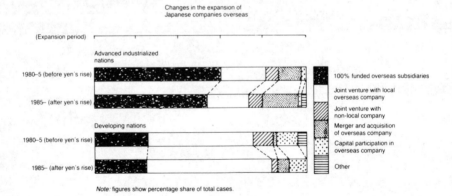

United States   Asian NICs

Manufacturing industries   (Expansion period)   Manufacturing industries

1980–5
(before yen's rise)

1985–
(after yen's rise)

Processing and assembly   Processing and assembly

1980–5
(before yen's rise)

1985–
(after yen's rise)

To secure stable supplies of raw materials and parts
To take advantage of lower labor costs
To expand sales channels in target country
To expand sales channels in third country
To strengthen the local after-sales service network
To acquire information on technologies and markets
To avoid exchange-rate risks
In response to trade friction
Other reasons

Notes:
1. Multiple responses were given.
2. Processing and assembly includes four categories: general machinery, electrical equipment, transportation equipment and precision machinery.
Source: 1987 MITI White Paper.

Changes in the expansion of
Japanese companies overseas

(Expansion period)

Advanced industrialized
nations

1980–5 (before yen's rise)

1985– (after yen's rise)

100% funded overseas subsidiaries

Joint venture with local
overseas company

Joint venture with
non-local company

Developing nations

Merger and acquisition
of overseas company

1980–5 (before yen's rise)

Capital participation in
overseas company

1985– (after yen's rise)

Other

Note: figures show percentage share of total cases.

APPENDIX 23: SALES DESTINATIONS FOR OVERSEAS PRODUCTION FACILITIES (PERCENTAGES)

	FY 1983	FY 1986
Local sales	66.9	54.7
Exports to Japan	10.9	15.8
Exports to third country	22.3	29.5

Source: The 2nd and 3rd Basic Surveys of Overseas Business Activities.

APPENDIX 24: TRANSACTIONS BETWEEN PARENT COMPANIES AND OVERSEAS SUBSIDIARIES (PERCENTAGES)

	FY 1983	FY 1986
Parent company to overseas subsidiary*	29.9	39.2
Overseas subsidiary to parent company†	20.9	23.4

* Sales to overseas subsidiary divided by the value of parent company's overall exports.
† Value of purchases from overseas subsidiary divided by the value of parent company's overall imports.
Source: The 2nd and 3rd Basic Survey of Overseas Business Activities.

APPENDIX 25: THE TREND TOWARD MULTINATIONAL COMPANIES

This trend toward multinationalism of companies can be broken down into the following five stages.

The first stage is the expansion of exports or trade. At this stage, all of the company's production facilities remain in the home country and the company is simply trying to take advantage of economies of scale. It exports its domestically-made products to foreign markets where they are sold via foreign agencies.

The second stage is the establishment of foreign sales offices. At this stage, all of the company's production facilities still remain in the home country while the company sets up sales offices abroad to expand and strengthen its local sales network, get a better feel for customer needs and improve its various services including after-sales service.

At the third stage, the company begins building facilities abroad for production and/or production technology development. Such foreign expansion can be divided into the 'passive' type which seeks to avoid high customs duties and import restrictions in the target countries and to maintain or expand local market share, and the 'active' type which seeks to reduce raw material procurement costs and transportation costs or to get closer to the market so as more accurately and promptly to meet market needs.

The fourth stage involves transferring a full set of management resources to the target countries. The full range of management resources includes production, sales, R & D and capital procurement, and the foreign offices would be given commensurate management and decision-making responsibilities.

The fifth and ultimate stage of multinationalization is where the company's home country headquarters pursues a global strategy and is managed in complete integration with its offices abroad. The company has placed management resources such as those described at the fourth stage in various appropriate regions around the world, and all of these offices and factories – including the domestic ones – not only act independently but are also integrated in an organic network that fosters more efficient management of company operations through division of labor based on certain processes or certain distinctive products.

Any company that has advanced to at least the second stage is generally regarded as a multinational company.

Currently, many Japanese companies are progressing from the third to the fourth stage, but in the future, as international undertakings further develop, they are expected to carry their multinationalization even farther, approaching the fifth and ultimate stage.

APPENDIX 26: RESULTS OF OPINION SURVEY ON HIRING OF UNSKILLED LABORERS

In the following 'A' means positive views and 'B' negative views.

1. General opinions

A: Even if it causes a bit of social unrest, it would give Japanese people daily contact with other cultures and would thus be indispensable for Japan's bona fide internationalization. From a global perspective, there is no reason why Japan should stand alone as a nation that is basically 'closed' to foreigners.

B: We can see from Europe's experiences that allowing massive immigration of unskilled laborers leads to very high housing, welfare and educational costs for second- and third-generation immigrants. Nowadays, the global trend is toward a closed-door immigration policy.

2. Relations with other Asian countries

(1) The chances of friction

A: With such a wide gap in income levels, if Japan keeps refusing to employ other Asians who want to work, there is sure to be friction.

B: If Japan hires other Asians to do the dirty work, naturally there will be some backlash in the other Asian countries.

(2) Practical benefits for developing countries

A: Immigrant workers in Japan sending money home would help improve the balance of payments in their home countries. Immigrant workers could also later apply skills and technologies they learned in Japan.

B: If the cost is the same, it would be more constructive to use aid and investment funds to create greater employment opportunities in their home countries. Otherwise, most immigrants would not want to return to their home countries and unskilled laborers are generally not very adept at learning new skills and technologies.

3. Employment gaps created during the process of industrial restructuring

A: Japan could improve its international competitiveness by allowing lower-paid immigrant workers into the country.

B: Immigrant workers would slow down the progress of Japan's restructuring in low-productivity sectors and would thus pose a problem from the perspective of the international division of labor. Bringing in foreign workers simply as cheap labor would be an affront to international human rights. And it would mean an even greater boost in the unemployment rate which is already high during industrial restructuring.

4. Responses toward the growing number of illegal immigrant workers

A: Even 'illegal' workers should not be forced to tolerate deplorable treatment. Japan should face the issue head on and improve the treatment of immigrant workers.
B: The first priority should be to crack down on the people who knowingly break the law by hiring illegal immigrants.

5. The possibility of an orderly introduction of immigrants

A: Japan can avoid social disruption by accepting immigrants in limited numbers and under definite timetables. One measure of social stability Japan could use would be to ensure that immigrants receive the same wages, working hours, welfare benefits and other social conditions as those received by native Japanese workers.
B: If Japan relaxes its immigration policy even a little, a whole new flood of aspiring immigrants will come knocking at the door. At the same time, such relaxation would lead to an exponential increase in illegal workers.

APPENDIX 27: SUMMARY OF THE INF DISARMAMENT TREATY

This treaty was signed in Washington by the leaders of the United States and the Soviet Union on December 8, 1987.

1. Structure of the treaty

Treaty main text, disarmament protocol, verification inspection protocol and memoranda on agreements.

2. Specified missiles and disarmament timetable

(1) LRINF (Long Range Intermediate-range Nuclear Forces, 1,000–5,500km): three years
(2) SRINF (Short Range Intermediate-range Nuclear Forces, 500–1,000km): eighteen months
Note: The treaty refers to LRINF as medium-range missiles and SRINF as short-range missiles.

3. Number of specified missiles (deployed and not deployed)

	United States	Soviet Union	Total
LRINF	689	826	1,515
SRINF	170	929	1,096
Total	859	1,752	2,611

Note: In addition to missiles, missile transporters and carriers, such as those used for missile launchers and mobile missiles, are also specified by the treaty.

4. Method of missile destruction

The specified missiles are to be destroyed through explosion, compression or combustion. However, during the first six months after the treaty's effective date, up to 100 LRINF missiles may be destroyed after launching.

5. Verification

The verification method will be on-site inspections carried out in both signatory countries and in the European countries where their missiles are deployed. These inspections will include a thirteen-year program of short-notice spot checks and inspections by monitors continually stationed at production facilities (such as SS-25 factories).

Note: The frequency of spot checks is as follows:

(1)   twenty times per year during the three-year disarmament period;
(2)   fifteen times per year during the first five years after the disarmament period;
(3)   ten times per year during the second five years after the disarmament period.

6. Term of treaty and effective period

The term of the treaty is indefinite. The treaty becomes effective from the ratification exchange date.

APPENDIX 28: DEFENSE OUTLAYS AMONG MAJOR INDUSTRIALIZED NATIONS

	1980	1981	1982	1983	1984	1985
United States						
Outlay ($m.)*	162,400	169,888	213,626	213,459	258,164	272,499
1980s	162,400	153,884	182,430	176,558	204,730	208,881
GDP (%)	6.0	5.7	6.9	6.4	6.9	6.9
Soviet Union						
GDP %	2.0	1.6	1.4	1.5	1.4	1.6
Outlay (rubles m.)	17,124	17,054	17,050	17,054	17,045	19,063
1980s	41,766	41,595	41,585	41,595	41,573	46,495
GNP (%)			12.0–17.0†			
Britain						
Outlay (£m.)	11,542	12,144	14,870	15,952	17,511	18,352
1980s	26,850	25,246	28,471	29,197	30,537	30,171
GDP (%)	5.0	4.8	5.4	5.3	5.5	5.2
France						
Outlay (FF)	111,672	129,708	148,021	165,029	176,638	186,715
1980s	26,427	27,069	27,626	28,097	27,999	27,984
GDP (%)	4.0	4.2	4.1	4.2	4.1	4.1
West Germany						
Outlay (DMm.)††	48,518	52,193	54,234	56,496	57,274	58,650
1980s	26,692	27,012	26,664	26,887	26,612	26,666
GDP (%)	3.3	3.4	3.4	3.4	3.3	3.2

* The rows in each country's section show fiscal-year outlays in the local currency (l.c., unit: 1 million), the fiscal-year outlays based on 1980-value US dollar, and the ratio to GDP.
† Based on Western estimates.
†† Excludes aid to West Berlin.
Source: Compiled from 'Military Balance, 1987-88,' published by *Asagumo Shimbun.*

APPENDIX 29: EXTRACTS FROM 'REPORT ON DEFENSE BURDENS AMONG THE US AND ITS ALLIES' BY THE US DEFENSE DEPARTMENT

A numerical comparison shows that the United States is clearly making greater defense efforts than the vast majority of its allies. In recent years, US defense outlays have corresponded to 6-7 per cent of GDP, while the defense-to-GDP ratios among US allies have been 6-7 per cent in Greece, 5 per cent in Britain, just over 2 per cent in Canada and Denmark, and about 1 per cent in Japan.

Among the nations included in this analysis, Japan, the only non-NATO nation in this case, has a very high per-capita GDP but ranks near the bottom in terms of almost every indicator of actual defense burden. This shows that Japan's defense efforts fall far short of shouldering what would be considered a fair defense burden.

APPENDIX 30: US CONGRESSIONAL RESOLUTIONS AND STATEMENTS FROM MAJOR POLITICIANS REGARDING JAPAN'S DEFENSE CAPACITY

1. Resolution requesting greater Japanese defense expenditures

It was resolved that Japan should increase its defense outlays to at least 3 per cent of GNP. This resolution was put forward by Representative Duncan Hunter (Republican, California) and was passed on June 16, 1987 by a House of Representatives plenary session vote of 415 to 1.

2. Resolution requesting that Japan and the NATO countries increase their defense expenditures

This resolution was put forward by Senator Kent Conrad (Democrat, North Dakota) and was passed on September 29, 1987 by a Senate plenary session vote of 90 to 4.

Statement by US Defense Secretary Frank Carlucci, October 30, 1987

'Japan's 1988 defense budget includes over US$2.5 billion earmarked for support of US troops stationed in Japan, which includes increased outlays for US military facilities, maintenance and labor costs. This amount corresponds to US$45,000 per serviceman or servicewoman, which is the highest level of host nation support in the world.'

4. Statement by Senator James R. Sasser (Democrat, Tennessee), Budget committee meeting, March 3, 1988

'Japan ought to be made to bear the burden of paying the rent on US military bases in Japan.' (Defense Secretary Carlucci responded 'Japan has constitutional restrictions on that, so it would be more practical for them to provide economic aid').

5. Statements by US Defense Secretary Carlucci (at House of Representatives Foreign Affairs Committee meeting, March 8, 1988)

'The Japanese government will continue to boost its defense expenditures 5% each year.'

'If Japan's defense outlays were suddenly increased to 3% of GNP, I wonder whether their forces would be able to remain strictly self-defense forces or whether they would gravitate toward offensive capabilities and activities.'

'Other Asian nations look at Japanese defense growth with trepidation lest it reach that point [where it moves toward offensive capabilities and activities].'

'Our [US] government is looking into boosting our financial support to the Philippines government, and is now talking this matter over with Japan.'

6. Statements by Senator Ted Stevens (Republican, Alaska), March 21, 1988, at a meeting of the military construction subcommittee of the Senate Appropriations Committee

'If Japan is not willing to make big improvements in its defense outlays, we ought to consider withdrawing our forces stationed there.'

'The Japanese economy is taking over Alaska and most of the United States, for that matter, so it's only natural that the Japanese government should foot the bill for the operating expenses and facilities costs of our troops stationed there.'

Assistant Secretary of Defense Richard Armitage responded 'There's no need for this committee to resort to Japan bashing'.

APPENDIX 31: COMPARISON OF INTERNATIONAL CONTRIBUTIONS BY MAJOR INDUSTRALIZED NATIONS: PERCENTAGE GNP IN 1985

Expenditures	United States	United Kingdom	West Germany	France	Japan
1. Economic cooperation	0.05*	0.81	0.92	1.74	0.84
2. Research and development	2.01	1.52†	2.69	1.87	2.51
3. Defense	7.12	5.21	2.65	3.29	0.98
Total	9.18	7.54	6.26	6.90	4.33

Note 1: 'Economic cooperation expenditures' are the total amount of capital sent to developing countries.
Note 2: 'Research and development expenditures' include cultural and social research-related outlays and excludes defense-related research.
* The US ODA stood at US$9.4 billion (0.24 per cent of GNP) and the flow of other US official funding reached US$178 million; however, the US private sector had a negative capital flow totalling US$9.3 billion.
† 1983 figure.
Sources: 'Development Co-operation 1986'; compiled from 'White Paper on Science and Technology 1987', Science and Technology Agency (Japan); compiled from 'The Military Balance, 1987-88' by the International Institute for Strategic Studies (UK), published by *Asagumo Shimbun*); Japanese GNP figures are from the Economic Planning Agency's 'Annual Report on National Account' and other countries' GNP figures are from the Bank of Japan's 'Comparative Economic and Financial Statistics, Japan and Other Major Countries'.

Comparison of international official-only contributions by major industrialized nations: percent of GNP, 1985

Expenditures	United States	United Kingdom	West Germany	France	Japan
1. Economic cooperation	0.24	0.42	0.62	1.00	0.27
2. Research and development	0.57	0.64*	0.98	0.78	0.47
3. Defense	7.12	5.21	2.65	3.29	0.98
Total	7.93	6.27	4.25	5.07	1.72

Note 1: 'Economic cooperation expenditures' are the total of ODA and other official funds.
Note 2: 'Research and development expenditures' include cultural and social research-related outlays and excludes defense-related research.
* 1984 figure.
Sources: Same as above.

APPENDIX 32: COMPARISON OF VALUE OF PRODUCT IMPORTS AMONG MAJOR INDUSTRIALIZED NATIONS

Country	Product imports (US$1m.)	vs. GNP (%)
United States	257,918.4	6.45
United Kingdom	76,950.0	16.75
West Germany	97,676.4	15.57
France	66,860.4	13.15
Japan	40,153.2	3.02

Note 1: Product import values were calculated based on OECD's 'Monthly Statistics of Foreign Trade, Series A.'
Note 2: GNP figures are from the Bank of Japan's 'Comparative Economic and Financial Statistics, Japan and Other Major Countries.'

APPENDIX 33: RELATIONS BETWEEN JAPAN AND THE DEVELOPING COUNTRIES (BY REGION) PERCENTAGES

	Asia	Latin America	Africa	Middle East
Bilateral flow of capital to developing countries in 1986	50	34	6	1
Bilateral ODA in 1986	65	8	15	2
Overseas direct investment balance as of Sept. 1987	20	19	3	3
Trade with developing countries in 1987 (export and import)	Ex: 73 Im: 62	Ex: 10 Im: 8	Ex: 5 Im: 2	Ex: 26 Im: 9
Trade with the world in 1987 (export and import)	Ex: 27 Im: 31	Ex: 4 Im: 4	Ex: 2 Im: 1	Ex: 3 Im: 13
Description	Note 1	Note 2	Note 3	Note 4

Note 1: Japan maintains particularly close political and economic relations with East Asian nations (the Asian NICs, ASEAN countries, China) and places the highest priority on this region.

Note 2: Although this region is one of the most distant from Japan, Japan has long had emigration ties with it (there are nearly one million residents and citizens of Japanese descent in Latin America) and Central America and the Caribbean are important trade routes for Japan. Recently, Japan has provided capital recycling measures to increase the flow of funds to this area as part of Japan's economic cooperation with the United States.

Note 3: Japan has never had very close relations with Africa, and recent economic troubles in Africa have led to a drying up of Japanese investment and trade there. However, in recent years Japan has increased its ODA to this region as part of its international contributions and cooperation with Europe.

Note 4: Since Japan depends on the Middle East region for 70 percent of imported crude oil, it regards this region as its 'economic lifeline.' Japan also values this region as an important source of overseas construction orders.

Source: Compiled from DAC statistics, Ministry of Finance statistics and trade statistics.

APPENDIX 34: COMPARISON OF TECHNOLOGY LEVELS IN JAPAN AND THE UNITED STATES IN VARIOUS FIELDS

1. Technological fields in which Japan and the United States excel

The United States excels in seminal, future-oriented technological fields such as basic and large-scale technologies.

Japan excels in technologies suited to the general needs of its population, such as production and public welfare technologies.

2. Fields in which the United States excels: those that plant the seeds for future applied technologies

(1) Large-scale technological fields (Japan leads the United States in eight of these fields, is about equal in seven, and lags behind in forty-three)

As for large-scale engineering fields such as aerospace, marine technologies, nuclear power, resource and energy development in general and other highly technical, large-scale fields, Japan has surpassed the United States in certain areas such as materials engineering, liquid hydrogen engines, light water reactor manufacturing and safety engineering, but still lags behind considerably in the more general large-scale engineering applications such as space stations, satellite delivery and recovery, nuclear fusion, radioactive waste processing, coal and gas liquefaction, resource exploration and ultra-low temperature and ultra-high pressure applications.

(2) Basic technologies (Here Japan leads in three fields, is equal in four, and is behind in eleven)

In basic technology fields such as bioengineering, new materials and basic information processing technologies, Japan has caught up with the United States in technologies related to the production of mainframe computers, but America still enjoys an overall advantage in areas such as recombinant genetics, artificial intelligence and database development.

(3) Fields in which the United States maintains a near monopoly on the market and where it has a strong lead in seminal research (see Note 1) (Japan is ahead in three fields, equal in two, and behind in twenty)

In fields such as civilian aircraft, medical and social welfare technologies and environmental monitoring, Japan has accumulated a wealth of relevant technologies such as artificial hearts and urban disaster prevention. But in general, such research begins in Japan several years after its origination in the United States, and this gap is not getting any narrower.

3. Fields in which Japan is superior – 'Need-oriented' technologies

(1) Development of products for the general public (Japan leads in four fields, is equal in two and behind in two)

Japan is clearly ahead in production and product-development engineering related to electronics products used by individuals and families, office equipment shared by office workers and other machinery that is widely available in retail outlets. Specifically, Japan was the first to succeed in the commercial development of such products as household VCRs, video disks, and facsimile machines.

(2) Production engineering (Japan leads in twelve fields, is equal in zero, and behind in seven)

Japan and the United States each have their own relative strengths and weaknesses in areas such as ceramics production for electronic engineering, semiconductor fabrication technologies, memory chip manufacturing technologies and LSI inspection technologies. Japan generally lags behind in design, materials, refining and precision control technologies and leads in reliability testing and automation technologies. If we also take into account Japan's dominance in production-level management such as in process management and quality control techniques, we can conclude that Japan enjoys an overall superiority in production engineering.

(3) Engineering fields that require large-scale funding (see Note 2) (Japan leads in six fields, is equal in two and behind in none)

Japan has achieved a very high level of technology in traffic control systems, public telecommunications infrastructure, dam construction and other engineering fields that require large-scale funding. Japan particularly excels in areas such as magnetically levitated (maglev) trains and large-scale residential construction. This gap between the two countries is expected to expand in the future.

4. Fields where the United States and Japan are roughly equal

(1) Industrial machinery fields (Japan leads in four fields, is equal in four, and behind in six)

The United States and Japan are running neck-and-neck in industrial machinery fields such as industrial robots, machining centers and machine tools. Specifically, Japan leads in control technologies, while America has the edge in design, adaptive control and ultrafine precision processing machines.

Notes
1. In civilian aircraft, medical and social welfare technologies and environmental monitoring, the users do not have a large store of technology and, in any case, these are fields in which those who lead in seminal research are seen as dominating the market. As such, they are 'seed-oriented' rather than 'need-oriented' technologies.
2. In the fields of public transportation and civil engineering and construction, the users (e.g. the Ministry of Construction, NTT and the Japanese Railways) generally have achieved a high level of technology themselves or, in the case of large scale general contractors, they pass on their accumulated technological expertise by the manner in which they send orders to manufacturers. In such fields, the research seeds and user needs are united. However, the user needs side probably has more power (for example, telephone exchange equipment and bullet train lines must be kept operational).

Qualitative comparison of Japanese and US science and engineering levels in specific technological fields*

Technological Field	SE	R & D	Sources
1. Large-scale technological fields			
(1) Aerospace			
Space communications (Communications satellites)	U	U	(a)
Solar batteries	U	—	(c)
Materials technologies	J	—	(c)
Relay equipment	U	—	(c)
Parts	U	—	(c)
Three-axis control	U	—	(c)
Structural design	U	—	(c)
Thermal design	U	—	(c)
Artificial satellites (Japan has 35, the US 1,082)	U	U	(a)
Satellite design	U	U	(a)
Body technology	U	—	(e)
Attitude control technology	E	—	(e)
Thermal control technology	U	—	(e)
Engine technology	U	—	(e)
Space stations	U	—	(e)
Assembly and development technology	U	—	(e)
Docking technology	U	—	(e)
Closed ecological systems technology	U	—	(e)
Rockets (Propulsion equipment)	U	U	(a)
Lift-off rockets	U	—	(c)
Jet engines	U	—	(b)
Liquid hydrogen rockets	J	—	(b)
Propulsion systems	U	—	(e)
Navigation and guidance systems	U	—	(e)
System technology	E	—	(e)
Recovery technology	U	—	(e)
Orbital delivery technology	U	—	(e)
Reusable spacecraft (e.g. space shuttle)	U	—	(e)
Aerospace/aeronautics-related technologies			
Titanium alloys	U	—	(b)
Superconductive materials	E	J	(b)
Liquid crystal displays	J	—	(b)
Ultra large-scale machining tools	U	—	(b)
Special-purpose machine tools	U	—	(b)
Numerically controlled machine tools	J	—	(b)
(2) Marine technologies			
Offshore petroleum production systems	U	U	(a)
Marine energy technologies	E	E	(a)
Marine survey submarines	U	U	(a)

(3)   Nuclear power

Nuclear fusion	U	U	(c)
Fast-breeder reactors	U	U	(c)
Production technologies for light-water reactors	—	—	(c)
Pressures vessels (output)	U	—	(c)
Pressure vessels (PS impurities)	J	—	(c)
Steam generators	J	—	(c)
Welding technology	J	—	(c)
Light water reactor design	U	—	(c)
Light water reactor safety	J	U	(a)
Uranium condensation	U	U	(a)
Radioactive waste processing	U	U	(a)

(4)   Resource and energy technologies

Oil sand and oil shale	U	U	(a)
Coal liquefaction	U	E	(a)
Coal gasification	U	U	(a)
Solar photoelectric power generation	U	E	(a)
Solar power generation	E	E	(a)
Wind energy	U	U	(a)
Geothermal electric power generation	E	E	(a)
Phosphoric acid-based batteries	U	U	(a)
Resources exploration	U	U	(a)

(5)   Extreme-environment technologies

Ultra-high vacuum	E	E	(a)
Ultra-low temperature	U	E	(a)
Ultra-high pressure	U	E	(a)

2.   Basic technologies

(1)   Bioengineering

Gene splicing	U	U	(a)
Animal cell cultivation	U	U	(a)

(2)   Information processing-related basic technologies

Database generation technology	U	U	(a)
Artificial intelligence	U	J	(a, b)
Pattern recognition	E	U	(a)
Supercomputers	U	J	(b)
Mainframe (general-purpose) computers	E	E	(a)
Logical device technology	J	—	(c)
Large-capacity DRAMs	J	—	(b)
Gallium-arsenide devices	J	—	(b)

Josephson junction devices	E	—	(b)
Operating system software	U	—	(c)
Design	U	—	(c)
30-kilostep class of packaged software			
Automatic software generation technology	U	—	(c)
Program development tools	U	—	(c)
Configuration management	U	—	(c)
New program development	U	—	(c)

(3) New materials

Ceramics	E	E	(a)

3. Technologies having limited markets

(1) Civilian aircraft	U	U	(a)
Engine technology	U	—	(c)
Engine design technology	U	—	(c)
Body design technology	U	—	(c)
Body processing technology	U	—	(c)
Flight-related aircraft electronics technology	U	—	(c)

(2) Medical and social welfare technologies

Pharmaceutical R & D	U	E	(a)
Development of new antibiotics and anti-cancer drugs	U	—	(c)
Toxicity testing of antibiotics and anti-cancer drugs	U	—	(c)
Clinical testing of antibiotics and anti-cancer drugs	U	—	(c)
Medical laser applications	U	U	(a)
Artificial hearts	J	J	(a)
Medical computer applications	U	E	(a)
Biologically compatible materials	U	E	(a)
Radiological measurement devices (Medical observation devices)	U	U	(a)
Digital radiography (X-ray medical examination systems)			
X-ray generators	U	—	(c)
Televisions	U	—	(c)

(3) Environmental monitoring and disaster prevention technologies

Measurement and analysis of atmospheric pollutants	U	E	(a)
Environmental impact evaluation	E	E	(a)
Global-scale atmospheric observation and measurement	U	U	(a)
Earthquake prediction	E	J	(a)
Weather forecasting	U	U	(a)

	Urban disaster prevention	J	J	(a)
	Safety evaluation of chemical substances	U	U	(a)
	Fire prevention	J	E	(a)

4. Domestic market-oriented technologies that require large-scale project funding

(1) Public transportation

Traffic control systems	J	E	(a)
Magnetically levitated trains	J	J	(a)

(2) Civil engineering and construction

Dam construction	E	E	(a)
Residential housing construction	J	J	(a)

(3) Public communications infrastructure

Fiber optics	J	E	(a)
Optical devices	J	E	(a)
Polarized-plane optical fibers	J	E	(a)
Optical communications	E	E	(a)

5. Product technologies aimed at open markets

(1) Personal (household) equipment

Video disks	J	E	(a)
Videotext	J	E	(a)
Multipurpose CATV	U	E	(a)
Mobile communications	E	U	(a)

(2) Group (office, etc.) equipment

Facsimile machines	J	J	(a)
Photocopiers	J	J	(a)
Laser printers	E	J	(a)
Microcomputers; personal computers	U	U	(a)

6. Production engineering

(1) Production equipment

Industrial robots	J	E	(a)
Servo motor technology	E	—	(c)
Control technology	J	—	(c)
Design technology	U	—	(c)
Software technology	E	—	(d)

Machining centers			
Servo motor control technology	J	—	(c)
Control technology	J	—	(c)
Precision machine technology	U	—	(c)
High-precision machine technology	U	—	(c)
Adaptive control	U	—	(c)
Design technology	U	—	(c)
Machine tools	E	U	(a)
CAD/CAM	U	U	(a)
Cutting tools	E	E	(a)

(2) Production technologies

Automobile engine parts	U	U	(a)
Fermentation technology	J	E	(a)
Ceramic electronic equipment parts manufacturing technologies			
Controlled atmosphere heat treatment	J	—	(c)
precision processing	J	—	(c)
Precision coating	J	—	(c)
Semiconductor fabrication technologies	J	E	(a)
Crystal growth technology	J	—	(c)
Stripe formation technology	J	—	(c)
Thin barrier layer technology	U/J†	J	(d)
Memory chips			
Crystals	U	—	(c)
Ion implants	U	—	(c)
Low-temperature annealing	J	—	(c)
Clean room technology	J	—	(c)
Reliability testing	J	—	(c)
Design	U	—	(c)
LSI probers			
Precision equipment control technology	U	—	(c)
Automation technology	J	—	(c)
Microprocessor technology	J	—	(c)
Pattern recognition technology	U	—	(c)
Design technology	U	—	(c)

* The 'S & E' column indicates relative levels of science and engineering, and the 'R & D' column relative R & D potential, with J, E and U interpreted as follows: J, Japan is superior; E, Japan and USA are about equal; U, USA is superior
† U for 1983 and J for 1982.
Sources:
(a) 'Comprehensive Survey and Analysis of Science and Engineering Levels and R & D Potential,' Japan Techno-Economics Society, March 1984.
(b) *PHP Voice*, September 1987 issue.
(c) 'Japan's Industrial Technology: Organization and Issues' (August 1983, by MITI's Agency of Industrial Science and Technology).
(d) 'Japan's Industrial Technology: International Comparisons' (August 1982, by MITI's Agency of Industrial Science and Technology).
(e) Independent surveys, etc.

APPENDIX 35: INDICATORS OF TECHNOLOGICAL LEVELS AMONG JAPAN, THE UNITED STATES, FRANCE, BRITAIN AND WEST GERMANY

	Japan	United States	France	Britain	West Germany	Average	Standard Deviation	Year/Source
1. Investment indicators								
1-1. Research costs								
Total research costs (US$m.)	33,490	88,330	13,134	12,550	18,130	33,127	31,998	1983 (a)
Rise in above (%)	14.4	9.49	10.8	5.06	7.67	9.49	3.50	1981–3 (a)
Portion paid by government (%)	24.0	49.1	54.0	50.2	40.9	43.6	12.0	1983 (a)
Rise in above (%)	−5.69	−0.122	1.05	1.21	−0.868	−0.884	2.82	1981–3 (a)
Private-sector research costs (US$m.)	21,820	43,250	5,511	5,283	10,541	17,281	15,991	1983 (a)
Rise in above (%)	17.0	9.70	12.3	6.08	8.71	10.8	4.16	1981–3 (a)
Per capita research costs (US$)	65,129	107,800	125,100	108,900	122,000	106,000	24,000	1981 (a)
1-2. Researchers								
Total number of researchers	392,600	683,700	85,500	104,400	128,200	279,000	259,000	1981 (a)

2. Result indicators

2-1. Science indicators

								Year
Number of published scientific papers per capita	250	373	277	333	302	307	48.0	1985 (b)
Rise in above (%)	6.91	3.78	3.37	1.70	3.42	3.84	1.90	1976–85 (b)
Number of recent Nobel prize laureates	2	33	2	6	6	9.80	13.1	1978–87 (c)
Number of research papers quoted in other publications	1,580	23,759	3,512	3,469	3,528	7,170	9,310	1982 (d)
Number of research papers quoted in other countries' publications	1,059	7,099	2,500	2,453	2,674	3,160	2,300	1982 (d)
Number of research papers quoted in developing countries' publications	182	2,936	529	658	608	983	1,110	1982 (d)
Rise in same (%)	2.28	1.80	1.15	1.41	3.62	2.05	0.975	1977–82 (d)

2-2. Engineering indicators

								Year
Number of patents received in other countries	29,170	54,460	14,770	11,674	34,744	29,000	17,200	1984 (e)
Number of patents received in developing countries	3,755	10,674	4,401	2,842	10,046	6,340	3,710	1984 (e)
Number of engineering research papers per capita	345	575	257	394	367	388	117	1985 (b)
Rise in same (%)	7.22	7.36	3.61	3.50	2.78	4.89	2.21	1976–85 (b)

2-3. High-technology industry indicators

								Year
Total value of product exports (US$m.)	170,500	145,300	73,710	67,930	161,600	124,000	49,300	1985 (f)
Rise in same (%)	8.32	1.28	1.67	1.38	1.93	2.92	3.03	1982–85 (f)
Total value of product imports (US$m.)	35,790	258,200	66,440	75,120	94,120	106,000	87,700	1985 (f)
Rate of horizontal division of labor (%)	34.7	72.0	94.8	95.0	73.6	74.0	24.6	1985 (f)
High-tech share (%)	21.7	38.4	8.90	7.80	10.8	17.5	12.9	1980 (a)
Rise in same (%)	3.70	−2.28	1.16	2.78	0.186	1.11	2.34	1975–80 (a)
Number of hi-tech fields in which country has relative superiority	147	156	83	118	82	117	34.7	1984 (a)
Rise in same (%)	1.05	0.001	0.612	−0.626	−3.10	−0.413	1.63	1980–4 (a)
Proportion of high-tech industries (%)	13.4	10.8	11.3	12.5	12.0	12.0	1.02	1982 (a)
Rise in mining and manufacturing industries (%)	4.30	3.50	0.10	−0.20	1.60	1.86	2.00	1977–86 (f)
Rise in productivity (%)	3.80	3.20	3.80	2.70	2.90	3.28	0.507	1977–86 (f)

3. Research base

3-1. Human indicators

Percentage of population receiving higher education

32.4	41.7	26.4	18.3	29.9	29.7	8.55	1983 (g)

Proportion of science, engineering, and agriculture undergraduate students (%)

26.5	20.8	22.1	35.9	20.7	25.2	6.43	1983 (g)

Proportion of science, engineering, and agriculture graduate students (%)

57.8	13.2	38.2	41.6	30.8	36.3	16.3	1983 (g)

3-2. Reference material indicators

Ratio of population to museums

5	21	16	16	9	13.4	6.35	1969–81 (h)

Proportion of pure science publications

6.48	3.70	2.75	9.04	4.64	5.32	2.49	1981 (i)

Proportion of applied science publications

14.5	9.92	14.8	18.8	12.3	14.1	3.29	1981 (i)

Number of books published

42,219	76,976	37,308	42,972	56,568	51,200	16,100	1981 (i)

Contribution to worldwide databases

3.00	49.5	12.4	11.0	3.50	15.9	19.3	1980 (j)

Expenditures to support databases

407	2,565	94	144	86	659	1,070	1984 (j)

3-3. Industrial indicator

Value of total scientific research-related equipment units shipped

9,742	8,532	1,518	2,300	3,941	5,210	3,720	1978 (l)

4. Exchange indicators

4-1. Technical exchange indicators

								1983–5
Total value of technology exports ($bn.)	1,724	20,301	1,021	2,214	1,301	5,310	8,390	
Rise in same (%)	4.47	5.33	−27.2	1.24	5.78	−2.07	14.2	(m)
Total value of technology imports ($bn.)	5,631	494	2,094	1,737	2,373	2,470	1,910	(m)
Rise in same (%)	4.26	−59.7	−3.58	−3.91	9.80	−10.6	28.0	(m)
Balance of technology trade	0.306	41.1	0.488	1.27	0.548	8.75	18.1	(m)

Guide to sources:

(a) From OECD's *Science and Technology Indicators '86.*

(b) *National Research Activities as Seen in Publications Data,* by the Japanese Ministry of Education.

(c) *World Yearbook 1987.*

(d) Excerpts from 'Survey of Conditions for Promoting Technological Development,' by the Institute Policy and Sciences, Japan, as quoted in 'Survey regarding International Distribution of Science and Technology Information,' by the Japanese Agency of Industrial Science and Technology.

(e) From Japanese Patent Office Annual Report, 1985.

(f) From the 1987 edition of *Comparative Economic and Financial Statistics, Japan and Other Major Countries* by the Bank of Japan.

(g) From 'International Comparison of Educational Indicators,' by the Japanese Ministry of Education.

(h) From Japanese Ministry of Education materials, based partially on the *UNESCO '81 Statistical Yearbook.*

(i) From 'Statistical Yearbook 83/84' by the United Nations.

(j) 'Databases in Europe: Today and Tomorrow,' by the Database Promotion Center, Japan.

(k) *OECD Machine Industry Statistics 1977-80,* by the OECD.

(l) Science and Technology Agency, *White Paper on Science & Technology,* 1986 ed, p. 386.

APPENDIX 36: JAPAN'S THREE PRINCIPLES ON ARMS EXPORT

1.Three Principles on Arms Export

In April 1967, Prime Minister Sato announced the following three principles regarding the export of arms from Japan. In principle, Japan will export arms to:

(1)   Communist countries;
(2)   Countries where arms exports are forbidden by a United Nations resolution; or
(3)   Countries that are involved or are likely to become involved in international conflicts.

2. Unanimous agreement regarding arms exports the Japanese government reached in February 1976

This agreement was summarized by Prime Minister Miki as containing the following three points:

(1)   Japan will not allow arms exports to countries indicated in Japan's Three Principles on Arms Export;
(2)   Japan will exercise the utmost care in exporting arms to countries not indicated in Japan's Three Principles on Arms Export; and
(3)   Equipment related to the manufacture of arms shall be treated as arms and in keeping with this policy their export shall not be encouraged. (Arms-related technologies will also be treated as arms.)

Index